This book is part of the Victor FAMILY CONCERN SERIES, a multivolume library dealing with the major questions confronting Christian families today. Each book is accompanied by a Leader's Guide for group study and a Personal Involvement Workbook for individual enrichment. All are written in a readable practical style by qualified, practicing professionals. Authors of the series are:

Anthony Florio, Ph.D., premarriage, marriage, and family counselor, *Two to Get Ready* (premarital preparation);

Rex Johnson, assistant professor of Christian education, Talbot Seminary, active in pastoral counseling, *At Home with Sex* (sex education and marriage preparation in the family);

Harold Myra, publisher of *Christianity Today, Love Notes to Jeanette* (sexuality and fulfillment in marriage);

J. Allan Petersen, speaker at Family Affair Seminars, *Conquering Family Stress* (facing family crises);

Nancy Potts, marriage and family counselor, *Loneliness: Living Between the Times* (dealing with personal loneliness);

Wayne Rickerson, family pastor, Beaverton Christian Church, Beaverton, Oregon and director of Creative Home Teaching Seminars, *Family Fun and Togetherness* (family togetherness activities);

Barbara Sroka, served on research and writing committees with Chicago's Circle Church and is active with their single adults, *One Is a Whole Number* (singles and the church);

James Thomason, assistant pastor at Calvary Baptist Church, Detroit, *Common Sense about Your Family Dollars* (family finances);

Ted Ward, Ph.D., professor and director of Values Development Education program at Michigan State University, *Values Begin at Home* (value development in the family);

H. Norman Wright, assistant professor of psychology at Biola College and marriage, family, and child counselor, *The Family that Listens* (parent-child communication).

Consulting editor for the series is J. Allan Petersen, president of Family Concern Inc.

The Family that Listens

H. Norman Wright

While this book is designed for the reader's personal enjoyment and profit, it is also intended for group study. A Leader's Guide with Victor Multiuse Transparency Masters and a Personal Involvement Workbook are available from your local Christian bookstore or from the publisher at $2.95 each.

VICTOR BOOKS

a division of SP Publications, Inc., Wheaton, Illinois
Offices also in Fullerton, California • Whitby, Ontario, Canada • London, England

Second printing, 1979

Scripture quotations are from the *New American Standard Bible* (NASB), © 1960, 1962, 1963, 1968, 1971, 1972, 1973, The Lockman Foundation, La Habra, California; *The Living Bible* (LB), © 1971, Tyndale House Publishers, Wheaton, Ill.; *The New Testament in Modern English* (PH), © by J. B. Phillips, published by The MacMillan Company; the *Amplified Bible* (AMP), © Zondervan Publishing House. All quotations used by permission.

Dewey Decimal Classification: 261.83421
  Subject headings: FAMILY RELATIONS; HOME LIFE

Library of Congress Catalog Card Number: 78-057370
ISBN: 0-88207-633-7

VICTOR BOOKS
A division of SP Publications, Inc.
P.O. Box 1825 • Wheaton, Illinois 60187

Contents

FOREWORD

Norman Wright is associate professor of psychology in the graduate department of family and marriage counseling at Biola College. He is founder and director of Christian Marriage Enrichment (Denver) and conducts marriage enrichment seminars about the country.

This book is a significant part of Victor Books' Family Concern Series. In a time of great family consciousness and opportunity, many congregations are devoting increasing energies to family ministries. They have requested reliable and practical resources that speak to the needs of contemporary families. Victor Books and Family Concern have shared this vision and have cooperatively developed this comprehensive family ministry resource for churches.

The church relates to people throughout their lives, and so can help them whatever their point of need. It can teach people skills and concepts for healthy marriage and family relationships with greater depth than any other institution. The church can offer assistance and support at times of crisis, and has built-in structures for education, enrichment, and problem-solving.

This Family Concern Series has been carefully planned to capitalize on the unique abilities and opportunities churches have to minister to families. These books are an encyclopedia of practical family information through which an individual can seek understanding. Pastors and other church professionals will find them invaluable for reference and counseling. Though each book stands alone as a valuable resource, study materials are also provided so that they may be used in church and group settings. As a package, the Family Concern Series offers the congregation a thorough, long-term plan for adult family-life education, and the resources for meeting the specialized family needs of its people.

The resources in the Family Concern Series focus on the needs of three audiences: single adults, never married or formerly married—married couples, with or without children—and, parents faced with child-rearing responsibilities.

Each author in this series is a committed disciple of Jesus Christ, with a concern for the local church and with a high level of expertise in his/her subject. I am pleased with the enthusiastic cooperation of all these Christian leaders.

God uses people more than books to change people, so this Family Concern Series has been designed to help people work together on their family needs A Leader's Guide has been prepared for each book in the series. It provides a group leader thirteen, one-hour, step-by-step plans for studying together. These may be used in adult Sunday School, Sunday evening or midweek study series, small informal study groups and as seminars and workshops in conferences and retreats. These Guides include complete study plans, learning activity instructions, visual aids, and suggestions for further investigation and reading.

In addition to the Leader's Guide, a Personal Involvement Workbook accompanies each textbook. This enables each individual, whether studying in a group or alone, to get maximum benefit from the study. Each Personal Involvement Workbook includes the worksheets and activity instructions that are used in the group sessions as well as additional exercises for personal growth.

In studying each book as a group, the leader will need a Leader's Guide and each participant a Personal Involvement Workbook. Even in studying on your own or with your partner, you may want to get the Leader's Guide and start a group study yourself. Use of the personal guide will increase the value of your time spent.

Since this Family Concern Series is a comprehensive resource, the needs felt by most families are included somewhere or several times in the series, even if the titles of the books do not indicate that. The chart on page 10 has been prepared to help you find these specific issues in this book and in the other books in the series.

To write a "family encyclopedia" would make for dull reading, but this chart is a guide to the most important topics in each book and works as an index to the entire Family Concern Series. To find what you need, look down the alphabetical list of topics on the left side of the page. When you find what you need, follow across the page to the right, noting the asterisks (*) under the titles across the top of the page. Each book indicated deals with the subject of interest to you.

This simple device ties the whole Series together. It is a road map that can help you get exactly what you need without being encumbered with a massive and complex index or cross-reference system. It also preserves the readability of the books. This chart plus the study materials make the Family Concern a powerful tool for you and your church in strengthening your family relationships.

A special word of thanks and appreciation goes to Norman Stolpe. As Family Concern's editorial director, he served as series editor for this project. His vision and relationship with the various authors enabled the concept to take form in reality. His hard work brought the series from planning to completion.

I trust God will deeply enrich your life and family as you study and grow.

J. ALLAN PETERSEN
Family Concern
Wheaton, Ill.

GUIDE TO CURRICULUM SUBJECTS

	Wright—Communication THE FAMILY THAT LISTENS	Ward—Values Development VALUES BEGIN AT HOME	Thomason—Finances COMMON SENSE ABOUT YOUR FAMILY DOLLARS	Sroka—Singleness ONE IS A WHOLE NUMBER	Rickerson—Fun & Togetherness FAMILY FUN AND TOGETHERNESS	Potts—Loneliness LONELINESS: LIVING BETWEEN THE TIMES	Petersen—Crises CONQUERING FAMILY STRESS	Myra—Intimacy in Marriage LOVE NOTES TO JEANETTE	Johnson—Sex Education AT HOME WITH SEX	Florio—Premarriage TWO TO GET READY
adolescent children	*	*					*		*	
birth control								*	*	*
child development	*	*			*				*	
child discipline	*	*								
child communication	*	*			*		*		*	
church-family		*		*			*			
dating				*					*	*
death						*	*			
divorce				*		*	*	*		
emotions	*			*		*	*	*		*
engagement							*	*	*	*
finances			*				*			
friendship				*		*		*		
goals			*	*		*				*
leisure					*	*		*		
loneliness				*		*				

10

1

Your Marriage—The Basis for

Your Communication

The little boy is tucked in, kissed, and prayed with. Teddy Bear in his arms, he is lying in bed thinking. He lives with his family in South America, and soon they are going to return to the United States. He doesn't remember enough of life there to know what it is like. But Mommy knows.

"Mom, come here, please."

She comes to the door and asks what he wants.

"No, come here."

She walks to the side of the bed.

"No. Come down."

His arm stretches up around the teddy bear to reach for her. She sits on the bed, coming down to where he is, and then he begins to pour out his questions about life in another country, his apprehensions about the unknown. Mom knows what it is like, but she has to come down, close, so that he too can find out.

This is a book about communication between parents and children. Your children can never understand all the things you do, and you may not seem to understand all the things they do, because you have forgotten what it is like to be a child. But you were there once. And when you come down, close, you and your children can come nearer to one another.

You might have expected to plunge right into the topic and begin learning the "how to" of communicating with your children. That will come, but first we should explore the foundation upon which parent-child communication is built.

Communication between parents and children is not a mechanical, rigid process like a computer program and does not happen because you punch the right buttons. Parent-child communication occurs within the natural process of family dynamics. That is why we want to look first at your marriage and your family atmosphere.

Begin with a basic premise: *The marriage relationship you and your spouse are developing will directly influence your relationship with your children.* If this is true, the elements of your marriage relationship should be examined.

Because the ingredients of a healthy and satisfying marriage are so many, only those that bear directly upon parent-child communication are discussed here. I am not suggesting that other aspects of marriage, such as finances, sex, and in-law relationships, are not important. The following areas were simply chosen because of their direct effect upon family communication.

In this chapter you will be considering:
   1. Your understanding of the purpose of marriage
   2. Your assumptions about marriage
   3. How your self-concept affects your marriage
   4. Love in your marriage
   5. Your expectations and needs in marriage
In chapter 2 you will be thinking about
   1. Handling differentness in marriage
   2. Decision-making in marriage
   3. Communication and conflict resolution in marriage

Before looking at your marriage, I want to share with you some of my biases about marriage, and also, what I believe are essential elements of an enriching and fulfilling marriage. Each Christian marriage has its own unique qualities. There is no ideal model for all marriages. Marriages cannot be stamped from a single mold. Within New Testament teaching concerning marriage, there is room for the freshness of expression and flexibility, according to the couple's needs, desires, and abilities.

A marriage grows best and produces best:

1. When the communication pattern is open and honest
2. When the uniqueness of each partner is accepted and encouraged toward growth, for the benefit of each one and the marriage
3. When decision-making and roles are based on each person's ability and giftedness and not on the expectations of others
4. When each understands and has learned to accept the purpose of marriage
5. When each has a healthy self-concept, and is able to be a giver in marriage rather than a taker
6. When each person develops the capacity to love— not a love based just upon feelings but also upon a commitment that tries to live the attitudes expressed in 1 Corinthians 13
7. When the wife and husband are not only lovers but friends
8. When a healthy pattern of resolving conflicts has been developed

Now think about these marriage ideals as you look at your own marriage.

The Purpose of Marriage

The basic beliefs about the purpose of marriage that two people bring into their marriage affect their relationship. What is marriage to you? I would like to suggest two definitions of marriage for you to consider. *A Christian marriage is like a school,* a learning environment in which both individuals have the opportunity to develop and grow *if* they so choose. One speaker phrased it this way: "Marriage does not demand perfection, but it must be given priority. It is an institution for sinners; no one else need apply. But it finds its finest glory when sinners see it as God's way of leading us through His ultimate curriculum of love and righteousness."[1] Do you think of your marriage as a curriculum? I'm sure you are aware of your sinful nature, especially as you see it sometimes exhibited in your marriage. Perhaps you can be thankful that, in spite of your sinfulness, not only does God love you, but your spouse does as well.

A Christian marriage can also be described as a total commitment of two people to the person of Jesus Christ and to each other. It is a commitment in which there is no holding back of anything. Marriage is a pledge of mutual fidelity; it is a partnership of mutual submission. A Christian marriage is similar to a solvent, freeing the man and woman to become themselves and to become all that God intends for them to become. Marriage is the refining process that God will use to make the man or woman He wants you to become.

I would like to focus on one phrase: *the refining process.* Have you ever thought of your marriage in this way? That God is going to allow certain events to happen in your life that will cause you to grow and develop into the man or woman He wants you to become? What would happen if you were to have that attitude toward the events that occur within your marriage—that they are something God can use to cause you to grow more deeply together, and also to cause each partner to develop as an individual?

Matthew

Each of us has had different experiences. My wife and I have had a unique situation in our relationship. We have two children, a daughter in high school and a son who is 10 years of age. His mental age is about 18 months and he will probably never be more than three or four years old. He is a brain-damaged, mentally retarded child. When Matthew was first born we didn't know this. At about eight months of age he began having seizures. We took him to the UCLA medical clinic where the diagnosis was made.

The name *Matthew* means "God's gift" or "gift from God." Matthew is God's gift to us. We have experienced times of pain, disappointment, and heartache, but we've experienced times of joy and delight. I can remember when we prayed for Matthew to walk. All of us in our family prayed for about three and a half years. One day when we were together he stood up and took about five steps. I said something like, "Isn't that great?" Then our daughter, who was nine years old at the time, said, "Let's stop right now and thank God for answering our prayer." It is interesting how our children teach us and urge us to give thanks to the proper person.

When you consider some of the events that might occur in your life, you could wonder, "How in the world would I ever be able to handle them?" But God gives us the resources to cope with whatever happens; He does this in His wonderful and marvelous way, even when we're not aware of it. God can be preparing us for situations that are later going to confront us.

Before Matthew was born I was in seminary. I had to write a thesis and didn't yet have a topic. A professor said to me, "Nobody's written a thesis on 'Christian Education of the Mentally Retarded Child.' You write it." So I did. I read books, studied, went to schools, and observed Sunday School classes for these children. What I learned about them I wrote into my thesis.

My wife typed the thesis the first time, a second time, and finally a third time, and she learned about retarded children as well. After it was finally turned in and accepted, I went to work part-time at my church while I was studying for a degree in psychology. There I was given the responsibility of training teachers to teach mentally retarded children within the church, so I had to develop a training program. During an internship in the public school district for my school-psychologist credential, I was assigned to test and re-test mentally retarded children.

One night two years before Matthew was born, Joyce and I were talking. We said, "Isn't it interesting—all the experience we've had with retarded children? Could it be that God is preparing us for something that is going to occur later in our life?" That is all we said. Two years later Matthew came into our lives. We saw how God had prepared us.

Response to Difficulty

Out of this experience over the past 10 years has come a new understanding of James 1:2-3. "Consider it all joy, my brethren, when you encounter various trials, knowing that the testing of your faith produces endurance" (NASB). "Consider it all joy" means making a decision in your own mind to look on an event as an occasion for joy. It means learning to accept what has happened even though it was not what you would have chosen if you had been making the decisions.

How you respond to difficulty, trials, and adversity can affect your relationship with your children. You can withdraw from them, be hostile and bitter toward them, overprotect them, or you can see them in a new light based on God's working in your own life. Your modeling of response will communicate a life-style to them. You may also face disappointments concerning your children's use of their abilities or the decisions they make for their futures. Will you be able to apply James 1:2-3 to these situations, or will you blame or question God? Do you blame yourself for the way your children develop?

Too many parents (even those who consistently provide the proper training and atmosphere) feel excessive guilt and blame. A child or youth, however, is responsible for his own behavior and actions. Consider what is said in Ezekiel 18:20: "The soul that sins, it [is the one that] shall die. The son shall not bear and be punished for the iniquity of the father, neither shall the father bear and be punished for the iniquity of the son; the righteousness of the righteous shall be upon him only, and the wickedness of the wicked shall be upon the wicked only."

Assumptions about Marriage

Along with beliefs about the purpose of marriage, you bring into a marriage relationship assumptions about husband-wife relationships. Take the following brief test and respond to the questions by answering either True or False.

	True	False
1. The longer a pair has been married:		
a) the more they will agree with each other.	( )	( )
b) the more they will understand each other.	( )	( )
c) the more accurately each will perceive how the other thinks and feels.	( )	( )
2. The more frequent the interaction between the spouses:		
a) the greater will be the agreement with each other.	( )	( )
b) the more they will understand each other.	( )	( )
3. The greater the agreement between spouses, the greater will be their understanding of each other.	( )	( )
4. The more democratic the relationship:		

	True	False
a) the greater will be the amount of agreement between the spouses.	( )	( )
b) the greater will be the understanding of each other.	( )	( )

5. The greater the involvement of the husband in his occupation and in the community, the greater will be the marital satisfaction of both spouses. ( )   ( )

6. The "happiest" marriages are those in which the personality of the husband and wife change very little, or if the personalities do change, it is in the same direction and to the same degree. ( )   ( )

7. For optimal marital satisfaction and adjustment, it is highly important that both husband and wife accurately perceive the other's role. ( )   ( )

8. Husband-wife consensus on such matters as religion, recreation, finances, philosophy of life, ways of dealing with in-laws, friends, and demonstrations of affection will not decrease with length of marriage. ( )   ( )

9. The longer a pair has been married the greater will be

	True	False
the amount of marital adjustment.	( )	( )
10. The longer a pair has been married the greater will be the amount of marital satisfaction.	( )	( )

Answer to Self-Test

According to research conducted by Richard Clayton, the answer to all of these questions is false.[2] More comprehensive research, however, must be done before these conclusions can be accepted completely.

Did you hold any of these assumptions about marriage? Perhaps you find some of them present in your life. But what about the assumptions you had about parenting? About how your children behave, look, play, and succeed in school? What about the assumption, "They'll grow out of this stage after a while and then I can relax"? What if that time never comes? Again we come back to the questions of how we handle situations when our expectations and beliefs are not fulfilled, perhaps because they were not valid in the first place. Will disappointments or changes of plans affect your marriage relationship and your relationship with your children? How you respond to these changes in your life will be your children's model for dealing with their own disappointments.

"How Do I Love Thee?"

As we consider the love relationship in your marriage, let me ask you a question: Do you love your spouse? Can you say with certainty that you do? Can you put into words what your love means? How would you describe it? Is it the eros type of love which is so strong at the outset of marriage—the physical, sensual kind of love? Is it the agape type of love which is the sacrificial gift patterned after Christ's love? Or is it philia, which is more of the friendship type of love? Love has many characteristics. Your marriage could have all of these kinds of love, for if each is purposely cultivated, it tends to reinforce and call out the expression of the other kinds of love.

Eros love involves cultivating the romantic, physical type of love through talking and creatively seeking ways to meet the physical needs of each other. This could include occasional honeymoon weekends without the children. (For suggestions in this area, read *Solomon on Sex* by J. Dillow. New York: Thomas Nelson, Inc. 1977.)

Friendship or philia love involves cooperation, companionship, and communication. It is not inappropriate for one's spouse to be best friend as well as lover. This is a biblical thought. "My lover, my friend" (Song 5:16).

Love also involves the agape desire to give something to the other person—desire to discover and meet the needs of one's spouse. This love shows interest, concern, empathy, and commitment.

Are you a giver or more of a taker? How would your spouse answer this? How would your children? Which of these characteristics are your children developing? Spontaneous giving does seem a bit uncommon today in many marriages, but it is essential. It must also be balanced with letting your spouse know what to do to show you love or fulfill your needs. Giving or practicing love and hoping to please the other does not have to be a guessing game, for you might lose.

Is the gift type of love present in your marriage? Think of your desires to give to or serve your spouse.

1. How strong and how frequent are these feelings? The servanthood role is especially important for men. The true meaning of Ephesians 5:22-23 does not grant them a dictatorial headship, but one of service.

2. Does the gift or service that you give to others cost you little or much? How is your life affected by meeting the needs of others, perhaps at the cost of your own? "Let each

of you esteem and look upon and be concerned for not (merely) his own interests, but also each for the interests of others" (Phil. 2:4, AMP).

Meeting Needs

A friend of mine has developed a procedure through which he and his wife meet the needs of the other. Prior to leaving his office he calls his wife and they discuss the kind of day that each has had, and then determine in advance whose needs are most pressing to meet that evening at home. Some days he needs to be left alone to unwind, or to jog for an hour to unravel the day. On other occasions her needs are more intense, and he may baby-sit so that his wife can take a long, leisurely bath. To some extent this would entail a denial of his own needs, but the amazing fact is that this is the best way of eventually seeing his own needs met.

The authors of *No Fault Marriage* had this timely thought to share: "The amount of satisfaction you get from your marriage is determined in large part by how well you and your partner agree to meet certain of each other's needs. It also depends on the degree of opportunity and encouragement you get from each other to meet some of your own needs." [3]

3. Does your desire to give come from a natural feeling of wanting to make the other person happy, or is there a sense of duty involved, a sense of "should" or guilt? You may face situations in which your feelings are not that strong, but if you remember that your behavior can change your feelings, you may approach the giving with a fresh attitude and discover some genuine feelings.

4. Is your giving string-tied? Do you set conditions or hold to some type of unwritten contract?

5. What is the purpose of your gift of love? Desiring to see the other person develop to his full potential and satisfaction would be an adequate goal.

The behaviors that cause love feelings are essential to the health of your marriage and your love. Edward Ford said it in this way: "It was in the very act of doing something with and for another person that you fell in love. It is in the very act of doing something for and with another person that you stay in love." [4]

These behaviors must be reinforced by approval to be maintained. For example, smiling, caressing, complimenting, spending time together, and helping with the baby are behaviors in marriage that may not be reinforced with appreciation. When these behaviors are no longer reinforced, they will stop. If your partner stops doing things that you like, your love feeling will disappear. It is important that you reinforce your partner for positive behavior (so that the behavior will continue) to insure that there is a continued basis for your love feelings. What specifically are you doing and what will you do to stimulate and reinforce behaviors that demonstrate your partner's love?

References

1. From a message by Dr. David Hubbard, president of Fuller Theological Seminary.
2. R. C. Clayton, *The Family, Marriage, and Social Change*, (Lexington, Mass.: Heath Publishers, 1975), p. 366-367.
3. Marcia Lasswell and Norman M. Lobsenz, *No Fault Marriage: the New Technique of Self-Counseling and What It Can Help You Do*. (Garden City, N.Y.: Doubleday & Co., 1976), p. 16.
4. Edward Ford, *Why Marriage?* (Niles, Ill.: Argus Communications, 1974).

2

Differentness and Decision-making

When you married, you were probably thinking about the similarities between you and your spouse. Now that you have been married for awhile, you have undoubtedly noticed the many differences between you. How you handle these differences is an important factor in family communication.

Differentness is closely related to decision-making. Differentness in marriage partners can be used to establish a pattern for making decisions in your family life.

Differentness

Differentness in marriage is important because it provides each spouse opportunity for need fulfillment. One of the main motivating factors toward marriage is a person's need to feel complete. Consciously or unconsciously you chose a spouse who you thought could help you feel complete.

Although this innate differentness can be a positive factor in a husband-wife relationship, it also contains seeds of hurt and disruption. You may be threatened by the differences in your spouse. You may be afraid that you will have to adjust your way of thinking and doing things. You may be proceeding on the theory that "If it's different, it's wrong!" You may also have some of these same feelings toward your children, especially if they start to show some of the "bothersome" characteristics that your spouse has! If you do not allow other family members to be different from you, minor differences will lead to major problems.

Abraham Schmitt described the phenomenon of differentness in marriage, the discovery of this phenomenon, and its potential for shaping individual lives:

In the midst of the marital struggle the honeymoon dream vanishes, and the despair over the old relationship comes up for reexamination. Suddenly each spouse turns his eyes away from the partner, and looks inwardly and asks, "What am I doing to my partner? What is wrong with me? What am I misunderstanding? What must I do to rescue this marriage?" If honestly asked the answers are not far behind: "I really married my wife because of her difference. It is not my job to make her over, but rather to discover and to value that difference. But before I can do that I must accept my difference and I really need her to help me discover my uniqueness. My task is not to mold her into a beautiful vase, but to participate with her to discover that beautiful vase, even as we discover it in me. How arrogant of me to think I could shape another human being! How humble it makes me to realize that I need to yield to another and thereby be changed! Our relationship will change both of us—in a process of being shaped into a form far more beautiful than either could imagine." [1]

Differentness becomes a problem in marriage when a couple's expectations about the marriage relationship and about each other are not fulfilled. Each person enters marriage with his own ideas of what the other should do and of what is supposed to happen in marriage. Sometimes these ideas are not very realistic. They may stem from television commercials or other media hype.

Too many couples build their marriage on *eros* love alone. Either there is not enough *philia* and *agape*, or the latter two fail to develop. In the delight of being together, and because of the sexual drive and sexual attraction during courtship, there is both a conscious and unconscious effort to ignore differentness. This ignoring of differentness may be called *selective blindness.* When a couple ignores differentness, they disregard or underplay the rough edges of differentness. Since they expect that an intense and automatic closeness will develop, they also expect that their differences will soon blend into this togetherness. Each person is, however, expecting to retain his own characteristics while the other takes on some of his characteristics and becomes a revised edition of himself.

Self-Concept

Each person comes to the marriage relationship incomplete in emotional maturation. Each expects completeness from the other. This need for completeness is a legitimate motivating force toward marriage, but sometimes this need is so great that a person sees in his partner only the differences that meet his own needs. He ignores the other differences. People with a poor self-concept tend to see their partners as more complementary than do persons with a healthy self-concept. How is your self-concept affecting the way you see differences in your marriage?

How you feel about yourself has a controlling influence on your mind and your behavior. A person's opinion of himself affects his interpretation of life, including his marriage and family relationship. If your self-concept is malformed, you will probably reject positive responses directed toward you. Your expectations may be unrealistic. Your trust level of yourself and others may be low, and fear and apprehension may be very strong. Often a person such as this is very pre-occupied with himself and does not accurately perceive the attitudes and concern that others have toward him. A person with a secure and healthy self-concept can accept change, others' opinions, and differentness without feeling threatened.

Especially during the first year of marriage, the ties we have had with other relationships are loosened and we think that all of our emotional needs are supposed to be met within marriage. Is this realistic? Too many rely on their spouse to meet all of their needs; they want to find their identity only through their spouse instead of developing their own personality! The togetherness that was so important during the courtship can easily turn into pressure during the first year. One of the discoveries couples make during this time is the shock of realizing that all of one's needs are not met by a spouse, and that one's spouse is recognizing previously overlooked areas of differentness!

Dealing with Differences

Thus we have some of the reasons for the problem. But consider this question: Why should couples be the same in every area of their life and agree on everything in their marriage? Why should they have expected that they would? Why should such an immense burden be put on the other to fill all of one's needs? The other person can assist us in the process of need fulfillment, but many people become too dependent. The marital disruption which occurs over differentness does not come about because of the differences. It comes because of a person's resistance to them, and because of inability either to deal with or accept them!

Steps to Healthier Communication

1. The first step in developing a healthier communication pattern in family relationships is to define our terms, using more affirming and less demanding statements, learning to make requests or complaints in a positive, specific manner rather than in a negative, general way. You need to accept the validity of others' viewpoints and ideas and then learn to mesh yours and theirs.

2. Identify specifically the areas in which each partner is

different. Then ask, "Why am I threatened by this attitude, belief, or behavior? Can it enhance our marriage, or is it detrimental to the growth of our oneness? Would I profit from changing or would our marriage be strengthened by each of us using our personal uniqueness together? Does our differentness reflect the fruit of the Spirit? (See Gal. 5:22-23.) Is it behavior that we want our children to have as a model?"

There are many areas of differentness that one can learn to accept. Others may need to be altered. For example, if one person is sloppy it would be best for him to develop self-discipline for his own benefit and that of his family. You can probably think of dozens of examples that will take some individual analysis and evaluation to determine if they are beneficial.

3. Ask yourself, "In what way is my partner's differentness (or uniqueness) related to his spiritual giftedness?"

4. Roy Fairchild gave some excellent advice to those who are bothered by the uniqueness of their spouse: Ask yourself, 'What would it be like being married to a person just like me—and would I like it?' "Differentness is another way of saying 'individuality.' We were created as irreplaceable individuals, different from any who have gone before or who will appear again. This is a frightening thought to insecure people who have not realized that God considers each person to be a talented individual of unique worth." [2]

5. Identify specifically your needs and your partner's needs and talk openly about how they can be met. Assist each other in the discovery process. Acceptance of one's uniqueness is the first step in this process.

There are five basic approaches which couples choose to deal with differentness:

1. *Surrender*—giving up and adopting the other person's ways.

2. *Subversion*—manipulating the person and using underhanded means of resolving conflict.

3. *Open warfare*—fighting over the differences.

4. *Negotiation*—giving a little to get a little.

5. *Self-change*—accepting the other person's differences, adjusting oneself to them, and making necessary changes in one's own life.

All of these methods can bring about at least some satisfaction, but only self-change can produce marital growth and complete satisfaction. This approach involves the application of Ephesians 4:2 to the marriage. "Living as becomes you— with complete lowliness of mind (humility) and meekness (unselfishness, gentleness, mildness), with patience, bearing with one another and making allowances because you love one another" (AMP). The latter portion of this passage, "making allowances," involves the acceptance of individual differences. The acknowledgment and utilization of these differences will be a powerful resource for the marriage.

Synergy

"Anthropologist Ruth Benedict often wrote about the 'co-operative energy' that flows like an electric current through a harmonious group. Similarly, two people working together can achieve more than either could individually using the same amount of time and effort. This effect is called 'synergy' —the enrichment, the added strength, the extra hidden ingredient that occurs when a couple complement each other by bridging their differences.

"Indeed, the differences are almost as important as the similarities so far as the synergic reaction is concerned. A traveler in a foreign country who fears or fights the differences in its culture does not enjoy his trip nearly so much as the traveler who accepts, respects, and even enjoys those differences. Much the same is true in marriage. If the two people are exactly alike (which, of course, no two people are but which some couples seem determined to become), they limit the potential that synergy provides. For differences add not only interest but also strength when both husband and wife have learned to deal with them." [3]

Ask yourself these questions:

1. In what ways are my spouse and I similar to each other?

2. In what ways are we different from each other?

3. For which of these differences have I thanked God?

4. How do my spouse's differences complement or help me?

5. Which of my own characteristics do I see in my children? How do I feel about this?

6. Which of my spouse's characteristics do I see in my children? How do I feel about this?

Decision-making

Who makes the decisions in your marital relationship? Who makes the decisions in your family relationship? Perhaps the question is not who does, or who should, but who is best qualified. Who in the marital relationship exerts the most influence on the other or carries more weight in deciding? What role do other family members have in making decisions?

Every couple directly or indirectly establishes a pattern for making marital decisions. Many of these patterns are ineffective or self-defeating. Some bring about lingering feelings of resentment. The majority of couples have not considered how they arrive at decisions. Respond to the following questions and then decide how well you have considered the decision-making process.

1. Who makes most of the decisions in your relationship? How would your spouse answer this question? How would your children answer this question?

2. Have you established guidelines to distinguish between major and minor decisions? If so, what are they? Who decided these?

3. What procedure do you follow when there is an impasse and a decision must be made?

4. How do you decide on responsibilities for household chores? How much say do your children have about rules for their life in the family?

5. In what areas of family life do you have the right to

make decisions without consulting your spouse? Who decided this policy and how was the decision arrived at? What decisions can your children make without consulting you?

6. Do you make the decisions that you want to make or the ones that your spouse does not want to make?

7. Do you have any "veto power" over your spouse's decisions? If so, what is the basis for it and how was this decision arrived at?

How did you do in answering these questions? Most married couples have never thought them through and yet they are vital to an understanding of the marital relationship.[4]

Principles for Decision-making
Consider the following principles concerning the decision-making process.

1. Are the responsibilities and control in your marriage divided on the basis of traditional role expectations, perhaps on what your own parents did? This seems a rigid structure in most relationships, but some couples find definite security within this system. However, when one partner begins to ask, "Why do we do it this way?" or when children grow up and leave, problems may emerge. The questions arise concerning whether the husband should be the one to wash the car and mow the lawn, and whether the wife should be the one to cook, do the housework and care for the children. You may find more creative ways of functioning than following the traditional roles. What examples are you setting for your children to follow? What do you want them to believe concerning a husband's and a wife's role? Work out a practical, comfortable solution.

2. Is the responsibility for making decisions based on your abilities and giftedness? If so, you probably have a very efficient marriage in which each partner is creatively growing as an individual. In this relationship, it is important that each person be aware of what the other is thinking, and the direction in which he is growing, so they can discuss issues knowl-

edgeably. What are your children's areas of giftedness in decision-making? In what ways and to what extent do you use their gifts in making family decisions?

3. Does one partner fail to assume responsibility for making decisions, thus forcing the other to make decisions? This has been called *decision by default*. Usually the one who is affected least by the decision allows the other to make it, but this is not always satisfactory. As long as one partner takes the abdicated responsibility, he reinforces the apathy of the other. It might be best not to take the responsibility so readily but to discuss the matter fully. Too many husbands turn the responsibility for child-rearing decisions over to their wives, but the Scriptures indicate that the father is to be involved with the child. (See Deut. 6:7; Prov. 1:8; 22:15; 23:13; Eph. 6:4; 1 Thes. 2:11; Heb. 12:6.)

4. Do you discuss together your methods for making decisions? If not, sit down together during a time when no major decision must be made and work out the process that you will follow.

5. If you and your spouse are using a set method for making decisions and it is not working well, experiment with another. Develop several different approaches.

6. Have you ever asked your spouse if he has difficulty making decisions? Is it easy for him? Does he know whether it is difficult or easy for you? You cannot always judge by his outward behavior. He may be experiencing some inner conflict and may welcome input from you. Have you ever asked your children if they have difficulty making decisions?

7. Have you agreed to make decisions in certain areas on your own without interference from your spouse? Many couples have numerous areas in which one is responsible for making decisions on his own. Some couples put a dollar limit on household or hobby items and do not have to consult the other unless the price exceeds the limit.

8. What are some of the major decisions that each of you makes? What are the minor ones? How do you feel about

these? Is there an area in which you would like some assistance from your spouse, or one in which you would like a greater voice? Some couples have written job division lists and have then considered who has the time, ability, and expertise to get each job done. They consider who is more concerned with each area and who enjoys the task most.[5]

Couple-Pace

In a marriage relationship it is usual for one to be quicker and more decisive than the other, and in the majority of cases the quicker decision-maker is at an advantage and his direction is usually adopted. The effect that this has on the slower person is that he tends to become slower and eventually give up. Why try? Thus he usually saves his response or reaction until the decision is made and then either shares approval or objections without having shared his thinking or reasoning on the matter. The same characteristic can be a problem when a child is slow in making decisions. His parents become impatient and then take from him his opportunity to make a decision. This denies him an opportunity to mature and teaches him impatience. Father Chuck Gallagher has suggested:

> We can influence the other person to make a decision by our rate of speed. For example, a fast person may come up with one solution after another and force the other person to take one or another of what is offered. The slower one may initially turn down all of them, but after a while feels that he has been too negative by saying no, no, no. So he says yes just because so many solutions are presented.
>
> On the other hand, a slow person can also exert pressure. He can give the impression that he is reliable, thoughtful, and more to be trusted in making decisions, thus implying that the other person is rash or inexact. The ponderous person can be so slow-moving—examining every little detail—that he frustrates the other party to pieces.
>
> A slow person can even put the blame on the partner when things go wrong and say, "Because you rushed so, you made me come to a decision when I wasn't ready for

it—I didn't have time to think it through."

It is better that there be a commitment by both spouses to get involved in the overall decision-making process. We have to develop a "couple-pace" of making decisions rather than maintaining our individual paces. The slow person can learn to go a bit faster, and the faster one can learn to slow down. The point is to formulate our decisions together.

Of course, we may differ in other ways in our decision-making. One of us may be sharp, clear, definitive and decisive. The other one might be cautious, gentle, investigative, option-oriented. Each of these qualities is good and has definite advantages. But if we maintain our individual qualities and don't mesh ours with our spouse's, everything imaginable can occur.[6]

Finally, it is essential to realize that the spouse who makes the decisions is not necessarily the spouse who *controls* them. Laswell and Lobsenz described the difference:

"Husbands or wives often 'delegate' decision areas to their partners so that while the actual decision is made by one, there is no doubt that the other holds the power. A 'helpless' husband may ask his wife to lay out his clothing every morning so that his socks, shoes, tie, shirt, and suit will coordinate. She *decides* what he will wear, but *he has decided* that she is to be his 'valet.' "[7] The key question ultimately is, Who decides who decides?

Finally we must ask, How is the decision-making process affecting the style of communication we are teaching our children?

References

1. Abraham Schmitt, "Conflict and Ecstasy—Model for a Maturing Marriage" (unpublished paper, n.d.).
2. Roy Fairchild, *Christians in Families* (Atlanta: John Knox Press, 1964), p. 149.

3. Adapted from Marcia Lasswell and Norman M. Lobsenz, *No-Fault Marriage: The New Technique of Self-Counseling and What It Can Help You Do* (Garden City, N.Y.: Doubleday & Co., 1976), p. 107.
4. Adapted from Norman Wright, *An Answer to Submission and Decision-Making* (Irvine, Calif.: Harvest House, 1977), pp. 50-54.
5. Adapted from Lasswell and Lobsenz, pp. 195-201.
6. Chuck Gallagher, *Love Is a Couple* (New York: Sadlier Publishers, 1976), pp. 76-77.
7. Lasswell and Lobsenz, p. 201.

3

Goals for Your Children

Young couples become parents for many reasons. For some it is "the thing to do." After all, most married couples have children, don't they? Some people become parents "by accident" because of improper planning or lack of birth control. Others become parents because they succumb to the pressure from their own parents for grandchildren. Some married couples want children so that they can have the opportunity to guide and develop a child into a purposeful human being. What were your reasons for becoming a parent?

No matter what your reason for having children, all parents face the same responsibility—that of guiding and developing their children to become functioning and useful persons. Have you and your spouse ever talked about goals for your children in terms of their own personal development? What do you want them to become? To test your awareness of your goals for the development of your children, describe what you want them to be like (behaviors, attitudes, skills, abilities, interests, etc.) at the ages of 5, 10, 15, and 20. If you have more than one child, complete this exercise for each one.

Many parents say, "If only they would 'turn out all right.'"

What does this mean? What is "all right"? Parents who have this as their primary goal are what we call *product-oriented*. They see their children as an end product. They feel that they have done a good job if their child is a Christian, attends church, achieves in school, produces results, etc. They have difficulty allowing the child to be a child and to make mistakes. Often parents are overly concerned that their child (or product) will reflect badly on them and cause embarrassment. You need to remember that there are no perfect parents and no perfect children. When you accept this fact of life you can relax and learn to enjoy others more.

Defining Spiritual Goals

One of the finest goals that you could set would be that your children would eventually exhibit the fruit of the Spirit in their life. "But the fruit of the Spirit is love, joy, peace, patience, kindness, goodness, faithfulness, gentleness, self-control . . . " (Gal. 5:22-23, NASB). Let's explore this further. Take each of the characteristics and define a general goal in relation to your children. Then give four specific examples of how you would like to see each characteristic exhibited or manifested in each of your children.

The second part of this exercise is perhaps the most difficult. What can you do as a parent to help your children reach the goals that you have defined? Naturally, having your children come to a personal relationship with Jesus Christ is the first step; but then, what can you do to assist your children to grow in the Christian faith? Give three specific suggestions for each of the qualities of the fruit of the Spirit listed in Galatians 5:22-23—ways that you can guide each child.

Emotional Climate

The atmosphere in your family life will be the climate for the growth of the fruit of the Spirit and also the basis for the type of communication that will occur between you and your child. This emotional atmosphere of the home is one of the most important factors that will affect your child's personality and his overall development. In his relationship with you, his parents, and with brothers and sisters, a child will experience what life and society is like. You as parents will build a family atmosphere, and in this small society a child will learn the economic, racial, social, and religious facts of life. Your child will absorb your values, mores, some of your beliefs, and will try to fit the pattern of standards that you have set.

The relationship between the parents can set the pattern for all of the other relationships within the family. This has been alluded to in our discussion of your own marriage relationship.

A healthy and Christian home atmosphere will provide the greatest opportunity for your child to develop into the person you desire him to become. What are the characteristics of a home in which a healthy communication pattern can be developed?

High Self-esteem

In the home atmosphere a central goal is to build the self-esteem of each person. This involves seeing each as being so precious that if he were the only person on earth, God still would have sent His Son, Jesus Christ, to die for him. It means seeing the value and worth in a person and treating him in like manner. Without positive self-esteem a person has a miserable time in life.

Self-esteem has a controlling influence on the mind. A person's opinion of himself affects his interpretation of life. A person who thinks unrealistically about himself does so because his self-concept is malformed. If it is severely malformed, he will reject even positive information and responses about himself which others seek to give him.

The individual who has high self-esteem feels worthwhile. He feels good about and likes himself. He accepts both his positive qualities and his weaknesses. He is confident but he is also realistic. He can handle other people's reactions, both positive and negative. He sets out to accomplish what he is capable of doing and feels that others will respond favorably to him. He has confidence in his perceptions, ability, and judgments. He is not afraid to become involved in the lives of other people or to allow others to become involved in his life. And he is not defensive.

Low Self-esteem

The person who has low self-esteem is just the opposite. He doesn't trust himself and is usually apprehensive about expressing his ideas for fear of attracting the attention of others. He may withdraw and live in the shadow of others in his social group. He is overly aware of himself and often has a morbid preoccupation with his problems.

Because he is so preoccupied with himself, he does not correctly perceive the attitudes others have toward him. He believes that other people must feel the same about him as he feels about himself. Since he feels other people do not want to include him in their group, he is hesitant to join them for fear of rejection. He can mingle with people but is hesitant to become honestly and openly involved with them. His avoidance of others has the effect of reinforcing his low self-esteem.

This individual is overly sensitive to criticism. He often attaches hidden meanings to conversations and situations. It is no wonder that people never get to know him or realize that he feels so bad about himself.

Foundations of Self-identity

Dr. Maurice Wagner, in his excellent book *The Sensation of Being Somebody*, suggested that an individual's self-concept (identity) is built on two foundations. One is called the *functional foundation* and the other is called the *feeling foundation*.

The *functional foundation* has three parts. The matter of

appearance underlies much of our thinking and conversation. The question we ask is, How do I look? How we view our bodies, our dress, and our personal grooming affects our appearance. How much emphasis does your child place on appearance?

The aspect of *performance* contains the question, How am I doing? This is how we view our abilities, skills, knowledge, and sense of responsibility. Does your child overstress performance? Do you, his parents?

The third area is that of *status*. The question here is, How important am I? We all want to feel admired and respected. Status can come from our family name, our education, position, job, and groups of friends we associate with.

These three parts of the functional foundation of self-image come from the way we feel treated by other people. When we are thinking of our appearance, performance, or status, it is as if we imagine that we are standing off and looking at ourselves from the outside.

The second foundation of self-concept suggested by Dr. Wagner is *feelings*. He noted three kinds of feelings that have unusual significance in forming the essential elements of self-concept: *belongingness, worthiness,* and *competence.* These three feelings constitute the mental structure of the self-concept. They support and stabilize the self-concept like the three legs of a tripod support its top. If any one of the three begins to weaken, the self-concept totters.

Belongingness is the awareness of being wanted, accepted, cared for, and enjoyed. Are you aware of being wanted? By whom? Are you accepted? By whom? How do you know? Do others enjoy you? Do you enjoy yourself? How do you know? Do your children enjoy themselves?

Worthiness is a feeling of "I am good," "I count," and "I am all right." People feel worthy when they do what they think they should. This feeling is verified when we sense that others have positive attitudes toward us. We look for their endorsement of our actions. A feeling of worthiness is related to a sense of being right and doing right in our own eyes and in the eyes of others. Belongingness and worthiness are similar. A person feels good about himself when accepted by others. When do your children feel most worthy? What do you have to feel worthy about? Who else sees you as being worthy?

Competence is a feeling of adequacy. It is the feeling of "I can," "I have the ability or strength to do it." A feeling of adequacy is built on present as well as past accomplishments. It is based on the achievement of goals and ideals that you have for yourself. Who sees you as adequate? When do your children feel most adequate?

Dr. Wagner described how these three elements—belongingness, worthiness, and competence—together form the self-concept:

Belongingness is fundamental. Worthiness somewhat depends on belongingness, for one must feel accepted by others to value their confirming attitudes concerning how good a person he is. Competence depends partially on belongingness and upon worthiness. We need to feel accepted by others in order to value their approval or profit by their helpful criticism. We also must approve ourselves to have the incentive to keep trying after we have failed. We tend to become listless and apathetic when we lose our sense of worthiness and feel like a nonperson, depressed.

Reviewing the essential nature of these three feelings, we observe these facts: Belongingness rests on the voluntary attitude of others as they display their acceptance. Worthiness rests on the introspective attitude of self-approval. Competence rests on the evaluations received in past relationships and on one's present sense of success.[1]

You may have built your self-image or identity primarily on what you think others think or feel about you. Is this valid? Can you always trust your perceptions of how others perceive you, or is there a better way?

You may have built your identity over the years by getting

an impression about yourselves from your parents or friends. You have also gone about confirming this impression. If enough people reaffirm what you think about yourself, this thought or belief becomes part of your self-identity. The problem here is that sometimes people agree with you just to be nice or because they don't care enough about you to confront you with the truth. Thus you get inaccurate information, build distorted self-images, and feel insecure about yourself. Some of us have lived in home atmospheres where we have received untrue information about ourselves because of problems existing in other persons. When you live with people who are overly critical and constantly putting you down, you may come to believe that you are "no good." This is one danger of basing the self-concept solely upon what other people say, think, or feel.

Three Equations

Many people have developed equations by which they attempt to become somebody. Drawing from the functional foundation of self-concept, you can develop the equation of Appearance + Admiration = Whole Person. But this does not balance, because you are not the sum of how you appear or what others admiringly think of you. Dress and looks are somewhat important but not to the extent that some people think. Many children and teenagers spend hours working on their looks and style in order to draw attention to themselves. They may ask others how they look, over and over again. When they receive compliments, however, they are not always satisfied, for if they were, why would they keep working and working on their appearance?

Another equation you might develop is Performance + Accomplishment = Whole Person. But you are more than the sum of your skills and the recognized abilities you have developed. Sometimes parents do not give love and acceptance unless the child achieves. Even then some parents may not give him recognition because, as one parent said, "I don't want him to become lazy and slack off. If I tell him that he did a good job, he'll get lazy."

Sometimes men value performance more than women do, building their self-concept on how well they succeed in their job. Their work actually becomes an extension of themselves. They throw themselves into it and spend many hours trying to achieve. But if their job fails, so do their feelings of worth.

A third equation is Status + Recognition = Whole Person. This equation is also untrue, for you are more than the sum of what people think of you.[2]

To become whole you must remember that you have been loved unconditionally and voluntarily by God, and that He has shown this love at Calvary. God declares who and what you are and asks you to agree with Him. Here, in His words, is the proper equation:

I created you and I don't make mistakes (Ps. 139:13-16).

You are worth the precious blood of My Son, Jesus (1 Peter 1:18-19).

I've adopted you and made you a fellow-heir with Jesus Christ (Rom. 8:14-17).

You do not need to strive to develop an identity because God has given you one. Is your child aware of the identity he has because of God's love for him?

References

1. Maurice Wagner, *The Sensation of Being Somebody* (Grand Rapids: Zondervan Publishing House, 1975), p. 37.
2. Wagner, pp. 162-163.

4

Family Atmosphere

A healthy Christian home atmosphere is one in which biblical teaching is applied and lived. Many people today know what the Word of God says, but do not demonstrate it in their daily life. For example, you are probably familiar with Ephesians 4:32, in which Paul says, "And be kind to one another, tender-hearted, forgiving each other just as God in Christ also has forgiven you" (NASB). Are these attitudes seen in your behavior within your home? What does it mean to "be kind to one another"? How can we show kindness toward one another in our family?

I remember an evening service in our church several years ago. This was a special two-hour service for all members of the family with a focus on family relationships. For over an hour we worked on the passage that I have just mentioned. I asked everyone there to write down how they saw themselves putting this passage into practice in their own home during the next week. They were given five minutes to write down what they would do during the week, and then I asked several of them to share what they had written.

Instant conviction took place when one lady stood and shared her intentions. In fact, most of the group recoiled as though they had been hit, for her application was one that almost every family needed. She said, "Well, this week in showing kindness to my family *I am going to speak to my own children as I speak to the neighbors' children.*" She hit the nail on the head. That *would* be an act of kindness. Most parents speak with more courtesy, tact, and patience to those outside of the home than they do to their own children. This is one way that a person can apply the teaching of Scripture as well as have it serve as a model for others in the family.

Love and Discipline

The healthy home atmosphere should be characterized by an abundance of love. The love of the husband and wife will set the pattern. The Apostle Paul instructed husbands to love their wives "just as Christ also loved the church and gave Himself up for her . . . So husbands ought also to love their own wives as their own bodies. He who loves his own wife loves himself" (Eph. 5:25, 28, NASB). Love also involves discipline. "If you refuse to discipline your son, it proves you don't love him; for if you love him you will be prompt to punish him" (Prov. 13:24, LB). A home without discipline provides little direction for the children. What does discipline mean?

Let's start out with the assumption that *discipline* and *punishment* are not the same. *Punishment* implies hurting someone in retribution or paying someone back for an offense. It is similar to "an eye for an eye." You punish to hurt another, to appease anger, or to satisfy the requirements of our society's legal system. Punishment can be a part of discipline when it imposes a penalty for undesirable behavior. But usually one punishes a child for one's own sake and not for the sake of the child; that is where punishment differs radically from discipline.

Discipline refers to acts or actions taken by someone in authority to restrain or rectify the behavior of someone under him. Discipline may include remedial measures, harsh or mild, that are taken to cause an improvement in conduct. These measures may be imposed in the form of precise rules or regulations to govern behavior. The words *correct* or *correction* are used in discipline; they refer to the pointing out of error in order to help the child as well as to change his behavior.

Dr. Bruce Narramore, in his excellent book *Help! I'm A Parent,* gave a helpful description of the difference between discipline and punishment:[1]

	Punishment	Discipline
Purpose	To inflict penalty for an offense	To train for correction and maturity
Focus	Past misdeeds	Future correct acts
Attitude	Hostility and frustration on the part of the parent	Love and concern on the part of the parent
Resulting emotion in the child	Fear and guilt	Security

You discipline with the intention of helping a person improve himself to learn a lesson that will make him a better person. You hope that your child will learn through the experience so that he will not repeat the act that brought about the discipline. In many cases the learning process will take some time. You also hope that your child will accept your rules and make them a part of his own value system.

Authority

Teaching must be a part of discipline. A person, in order to be receptive to learning, must see the teacher as having authority. Do your children see you as an authority? I'm not talking about an authoritarian person. That is different from an authority. You might ask your children or teens what they feel is the difference between the two words. An authoritarian person instills fear in others, does not listen to others or take into account others' wishes, and rules with an iron hand in a dominating, harsh, rigid manner. An authority knows what he or she is talking about, is a consistent source of information, and is a specialist.

One of the first and kindest acts in disciplining any child is to teach him that there is authority in this world. At times this authority has to rule without explanation. A young child should learn to accept the authority of his parents. His safety and his welfare depend on being obedient to them. There are occasions when time does not permit an explanation, or when the child could not really grasp an explanation if it were given. When a mother cries out, "Stop!" to a boy about to run into the path of a car, she wants him to stop immediately, without waiting for reasons. When a father counsels his daughter not to get into a car with strangers, he cannot burden her young mind with all the things those strangers might do. As the child grows older he will begin to ask questions, and as his reasoning develops so that he can handle explanations, more and more information will be given to him. But in the beginning he needs to see his parents as authorities, as teachers.

Trust

Children need good teachers. A good teacher is one whose teaching can be trusted. *A child needs to learn that he can trust the teaching of his parents. Parents must establish early in a child's life the dependability of their word.* Then the child will have a greater sense of security and will be on the way toward developing a healthy self-concept. In addition, a reliable trust relationship between parent and child makes it easier for the child to enter into a trust relationship with the Lord. Your child needs to be able to say, "My parents always mean what they say; I can rely on that!" This trust on the human level helps the child learn that he can rely upon what God says in His Word.

Necessity of Discipline

The Word of God tells us that we should discipline our children. Bruce Narramore illustrated it in this way:

> Since children are born without knowledge and with a bent to evil, it was necessary for God to provide a way of training each new member of society. A child's old sinful nature doesn't magically pass away. It must be controlled, disciplined, and eventually yielded to the new influence of the Holy Spirit. To accomplish this task, God gave kids parents! There are a few biblical passages on the necessity and responsibility for parental discipline!
>
> "And now a word to you parents. Don't keep on scolding and nagging your children, making them angry and resentful. Rather, bring them up with the loving discipline the Lord Himself approves, with suggestions and godly advice" (Eph. 6:4, LB).
>
> "Withhold not correction from the child; for if thou beatest him with the rod, he shall not die. Thou shalt beat him with the rod, and shalt deliver his soul from hell" (Prov. 23: 13-14, KJV). In other words, discipline is for our children's good. It is essential if our children are to live happy lives on earth and also be prepared for heaven.[2]

Encouragement and Openness

A spirit of encouragement and helpfulness to one another is essential. Children thrive on encouragement. It is a part of our response to one another as Christians. "Therefore encourage one another, and build up one another . . ." (1 Thes. 5:11, NASB).

In a healthy family atmosphere emotions are displayed freely, accepted, and encouraged. Children should be taught at an early age that emotions are a gift from God and they should be taught also about the origin of emotions, their purpose, and their proper expression.

Another mark of this atmosphere is open and honest communication. Ephesians 4:15 commands us to speak the truth in love. We are admonished in Proverbs 28:23 to speak to the point: "He who rebukes a man will afterward find more favor than he who flatters with the tongue" (NASB).

This is a home in which there is guidance and direction, but not an authoritarian atmosphere. Dr. David Augsburger described this feature in terms of autocratic and Christocratic personalities:[3]

The Autocratic Personality	The Christ-ocratic Personality
gives orders without asking questions, without permitting questions;	asks questions, seeks to truly hear, suggests alternatives;
makes demands, dishes out directives, lays down the law, defensive if challenged;	respects freedom and dignity of others, can affirm the truth clearly and concretely, but nondefensively;
requires compliance regardless of consent or agreement;	values willing cooperation, works for open agreement and understanding;
pushes and manipulates one-man rule in over-under position;	leads, attracts, persuades personal relationships in side-by-side identification;

says "you do, you must do, you ought to have done, you'd better do";	says "come, let's do, we might have done, can we try?"
depends on his own external authority to motivate others;	depends on his internal integrity to motivate others;
generates friction, resistance, and resentment	generates acceptance, cooperation, and reconciliation;
separates and isolates people.	unites and helps persons relate to one another.

Freedom for Growth

Family members need freedom to grow and become independent persons through discovering their own potential and spiritual giftedness. Paul, in Ephesians 4:2, describes some of the behaviors that encourage freedom for growth: "Living as becomes you—with complete lowliness of mind (humility) and meekness (unselfishness, gentleness, mildness), with patience, bearing with one another and making allowances because you love one another" (AMP).

The Scriptures also speak to parents of nurturing their children. The word *nurture* or *nourish* means giving the object the best possible care. It does not mean that you give enough barely to sustain, but that you go out of your way to give the best possible care so that the child can develop to his fullest potential. You ought to provide your children with resources and experiences so they can develop to their maximum possibilities.

Unfortunately there are some homes in which the parents are insecure and become threatened when their children begin the normal process of expressing their independence. Often they try to convince their children that they cannot survive without the parents' support or knowledge in making decisions for them. One of the basic principles for healthy child adjustment is for parents to "let go and let grow"!

You see, parents are the ones to set the tone of the family life. You parents have more resources available because of your age, maturity, experience and skill. Children and even teenagers should not be the ones who control the atmosphere. "If only my child weren't the way he is, we would have a peaceful and happy home," is often said, but it is not accurate. A family member may not be contributing to the happiness or peacefulness, but are you as parents allowing him to control you and everyone else too? Do you allow a negative person to sour the entire atmosphere? It does not have to happen. It is possible for you, as parents, to set the tone in the midst of upsetting experiences.

Respect

Respect for the rights of other family members is important. Parents have rights and expectations; so do children. A child has the right to expect:

1. A father and mother who love each other and show it daily in small ways and big ways.

2. Two persons who place on their list of priorities God first, then each other, and their children next.

3. Two interested, kind, and loving guides. Two examples, not perfect, but good.

4. Parents who put relationships first, always (before rules, what others may think, etc.).

5. Enough time in the average week with parents (actually there, in person) to build a relationship. Regular times to talk (one-to-one).

6. To be allowed to be a child. The right to feel and think as an individual.

7. Expressed affection, appreciation, and respect.

8. The feeling of being understood. It is often difficult for parents to accept and understand why what is serious to parents cannot be as serious to children.

9. Consistent, reinforcing acceptance. To be treated as a

valuable, capable human being. Never being torn down, never being attacked personally.

10. To be listened to always (not unhearing anger or patient endurance until you can "tell them a thing or two").

11. Parents who never treat lightly what is important to a child.

12. An attractive home—one of order and tranquility (that is, most of the time).

13. The right to privacy.

14. Guidance in forming good health habits. (Being overweight is more than just a physical burden to bear.)

15. Information about God, the Bible, a relationship with Christ, life, worthy goals, values, standards, sex, morals, alcohol, and drugs.

16. A single standard for both parents and the children regarding alcohol, drugs, honesty, church attendance, etc.

Attention-getting Mechanisms

If a child is raised in a home in which these characteristics are lacking, he does not have as great an opportunity to develop a healthy self-image. In fact, a lack of these factors can help to create a poor self-concept. A child in such a home may become discouraged. Often he will have a *desire for undue attention*. He begins to believe that he has meaning or value only when he is the center of attention. He begins to develop a repertoire of attention-getting mechanisms, including becoming witty, cute, or obnoxious. Some children find that attention derived through negative means is better than no attention at all. Many disturbing methods such as whining, teasing, dawdling, and spilling food can come about. Many parents fall into the trap of responding. When a parent gives in to these excessive demands for attention, he just reinforces the child's mistaken self-concept.

Other children may respond with a *power struggle*. If a child cannot get the attention he wants, he may decide to defeat his parents by using power. His satisfaction comes from refusing to do what the parents want him to do. If he were to give in to his parents, then he would be giving in to a stronger power and thus lose his sense of personal value.

A third approach, which is the result of intensifying the power contest, is *retaliation and revenge.* Some children choose this approach as their only means of feeling significant and important. They feel that they count only when they can get back at others.

The totally discouraged child chooses another approach. He demonstrates his *complete inadequacy.* He gives up completely. Why try when he has no chance to succeed? He begins to act helpless and uses this tactic to avoid any activity or task where he might show his failure and increase his embarrassment.

It is important to notice what your child is doing. Then if these behaviors are evident, action can be taken. (Note: These principles are expanded and many suggestions are offered in the book *Children: The Challenge* by Rudolf Dreikurs and Vicki Soltz (New York: Hawthorne, 1964).

References

1. Bruce Narramore, *Help! I'm a Parent* (Grand Rapids: Zondervan Publishing House, 1972), p. 41.
2. Narramore, p. 35.
3. David Augsburger, *Cherishable Love and Marriage* (Scottdale, Pa.: Herald Press, 1976), pp. 106-7.

5

Your Child and How He Learns

Your child is in the process of unfolding and growing. He is learning many things about himself and about life. As parents, you care deeply about his learning process. For you to help your child learn in any area of life, it is important that you understand how a child learns and thinks.

Children do not think like adults. Even though they make adult responses at times, they usually respond as children. This is normal, natural, and good. It is important therefore not to say that your child is wrong, illogical, or impudent when he makes childish statements. For his age, he is right. It would be helpful if parents could enter once again into the mind of a child and live there for a while, until they could feel what it is like to think and perceive as a child.

Perception—Seeing

A child's perception is different than an adult's. *A child may not see what adults see.* Children are shorter than adults, and because they are, they see things differently. Take an hour to walk around on your knees. What is it like? Are the houses larger? The table bigger? The dog taller? Some of the objects appear to take on a different shape as well. When you stand up again, you notice the same objects, but now they have a different effect on you. Because of your past knowledge you also know that most people are a certain size, dogs a certain size, etc.; but a child does not have this backlog of experience.

Imagine a three-year-old child who is seeing snow for the first time. She has heard about it but now actually sees the snowflakes falling. Depending on her past experiences, she may call them different names. One child thought they were frosted flakes, since she had eaten those and knew what they were. As parents, you need to know what your children are seeing and responding to, so that you may really communicate with them.

Children need opportunity to communicate with their parents. In *How to Raise a Human Being,* Dr. Lee Salk and Rita Kramer discussed the tendency of some parents to anticipate the desires of their children and to respond to these anticipated desires before the children themselves have a chance to express them verbally. By waiting for children to express themselves, parents teach them that speech is the means of precise communication. While a mere noise or body movement will get another's attention, speech is required to communicate specific desires.

You can stimulate the development of speech by encouraging your child's perception of differences. At first he will respond only to differences in the way things feel and move. Later he will begin to respond to verbal stimuli as he learns to attach names to objects and then to further identify them by adjectives that describe the properties of the objects.

Children enjoy immensely the acquisition of language skills. If encouraged, they will learn to use speech to describe and thus understand themselves as well as other people. If stifled, they may be inhibited in their adult lives by not seeing language as an acceptable means to define and express their feelings.

Sometimes a child's thoughts have a magical quality. A

four-year-old wanted to play the piano, so her mother got a book of music and opened it to a page that had a song her child was familiar with. She sat down and held her fingers over the keys and waited. She waited and waited for the music to happen. That child thought that this was how music was produced—opening the book and holding one's fingers over the keyboard. At one time she must have watched some-one playing the piano but she saw something different than adults see. This example is a natural learning opportunity. Too often parents ridicule or become angry and upset with the child's misperceptions.

Another reason why a child's perception may be different is that *children may see what adults see but respond differently.* Your child lives in the same house with you, but if you asked him to draw the floor plan of the house, it would look far different than the actual plan (and not just because of his lack of drawing skill). One explanation might be that children do not see the same distinctions that adults do. Or if they see them, they respond differently because they don't place the same degree of importance on the differences they see.

For adults, changes in their perceptions of an object do not change the object. For children, changes in the perception of an object may mean a change in the object itself. A four-year-old once asked his mother to make his favorite bologna sandwich for lunch. His mother had always cut the sandwich horizontally, but this day she cut it diagonally. The boy started to cry and said, "I asked you to make me a bologna sandwich, and you didn't." His mother tried to explain that she had indeed made a bologna sandwich. She had used two pieces of bread, some butter and mayonnaise, and a slice of bologna. She went over and over this, but her son would not accept the sandwich as bologna unless it were cut in the "right" way. Some parents would have blown their stack in this encounter and become enraged at the "stubbornness of the child." It isn't a matter, however, of being stubborn or obstinate. It's a child's world, and as parents you will com-

municate better if you remember who it is you are communicating with.

Perception-hearing

Not only do children perceive things differently, but they also
hear things differently. *A child may not hear what adults
hear.* You know better what words mean and how they should
sound because you can read. A small child cannot. You have
probably heard children give different phrasing for hymns or
songs sung in church such as "Round John Virgin" or
"Gladly the cross-eyed bear."

Children also hear words as adults hear them but give
different meanings to them. A Sunday School teacher once
called in the home of one of her three-year-old students.
The mother told her child that the teacher was coming to see
her. After the teacher arrived the three-year-old came walking into the room stark naked. In response to her mother's
frantic response the child said, "You said the teacher was
coming to *see* me." She had taken it literally. Make a list of
some of the words you use in the presence of your children
and then ask them what they think the words mean. Very
casually we use words such as died, kill, and smash; and
phrases such as "I died laughing" or "you killed me last
time we played tennis." What do these mean to a child?

Also, children understand concepts at different levels than
adults. They cannot deal with abstractions or the unseen. If
you were to ask several young children where babies come
from, what happens in death, or the meaning of *good,* you
would hear as many inaccurate or humorous responses. And
even when you help a child respond correctly, because of his
limited understanding and knowledge, what he does with his
answer will be different than what you would.

There is more to communication than just learning words.
If you studied a foreign language and learned only the
vocabulary, you still would not know the language. There
are other elements such as appropriate word endings and

sentence construction. Children seem to catch on to sentence construction quite easily even though they leave out many of the words that adults use. In most homes a child's speech is rarely corrected and when it is there seems to be little effect on the child. Most corrections that parents make do not concern the grammar but rather the truth or falsity of the statement. Most parents do not consciously teach speech or grammar to their children. Researchers now are suggesting that children have some type of built-in language learning system.

How then should you respond to the mistakes your children make in speaking? According to Dr. Silas Warner and Edward Rosenberg, "Acceptance and encouragement for what he has done, rather than correction for what he cannot yet do, are the best possible responses for parents." [2] They suggested a proper response to a child complaining, "Kitty scratch." The parent could say, "No, you should say, 'The kitty scratched me,'" but the child would not understand the difference and he might even feel that the parent didn't care about his hurt. If, however, the parent comforts the child and explains in his normal, everyday way, why kittens scratch, the child will feel that the parent is concerned. Proper speech will develop with time as he hears it from adults.

Communication Instruction

The development of communication has its basis within the home. Your child will acquire his speaking and listening patterns at home. How well he learns to use language will have an effect on his educational development, his comprehension development, his emotional development, and even his spiritual development. As parents, therefore, you can:

1. Speak correctly and distinctly.

2. Use proper grammar and words that are clearly understood.

3. Regularly use new words around your children in order to enrich their experience.

4. Gently correct defects in speech and errors in grammar. Don't laugh at mistakes as that will encourage some poor speaking habits. Baby talk should not be repeated by parents or grandparents. You may need to share with your own parents some guidelines as well.

5. A child should be spoken to in well-enunciated syllables so he can hear words distinctly.

6. Constantly attempt to build vocabulary.

7. Remember how a child thinks and hears, and accept him as a child.

8. Assist your child in learning to read as early as possible. As he learns the printed word, life can become much more real to him and his perception can develop. Both mother and father should be involved in reading to him and with him and listening to him read.

9. As your child progresses in school, help him by providing pleasant surroundings for reading and studying. Help him spend time each day in relaxed reading. There are many fine Christian books and secular novels and classics available.[3]

Parents Are Teachers

Remember that a parent is not only a parent but a teacher. If you are a teacher, you need to remember how children learn. Consider these principles:

1. Children learn by imitation. Those of us who have been involved over the years in the training of teachers and counselors have learned that others will not learn how to teach as we have *told* them to. They learn how to teach as they have been *shown*. We as teachers or parents are models. Therefore we should do the things we want our children to do and shouldn't do the things that we do not want them to do.

Earlier we were talking about reading. A boy is more likely to appreciate the value of books if he sees his father reading. Unfortunately those classified as readers today are women, not men. Some publishers of Christian books are hesitant to publish books for men because men are a minority in terms of purchasing and reading the books. It has been estimated that approximately 80 percent of those who purchase books from Christian bookstores are women.

I devour books—textbooks and books on marriage and family—but I also read adventure novels and especially westerns. My desire for books began in my home. My father, who completed only the eighth grade, read six to eight books every two weeks and he encouraged me to enjoy books. By junior high I had read scores and scores of books from our public library. I had a good model for this.

2. Individuals learn better when they ask to be taught something. Studies on learning indicate that teachable moments occur when a person is trying to solve a problem, when he has a need in his life, and when he is searching for meaning in life. Can you stimulate your child to ask you questions? Can you create curiosity in his life? Can you give him wide and varied experiences that will feed the native curiosity with which he was created?

When you stimulate your children to ask questions, then take the time to answer the questions. Why is it that some parents resent questions? They need to be asked and they are important for learning, and for increasing a child's communication skills.

3. For children, learning is more likely to occur when the learning activity is enjoyable or has an obvious purpose in it. As parents we need to stretch our imaginations to create stimulating experiences.

4. Children and adults learn more easily if learning has immediate meaning. Children find it hard to delay rewards or goals, and they learn more easily when they are rewarded immediately. No matter what your child does correctly, positive reinforcement such as praise, a look, or a comment will tend to bring back that positive behavior again.

Have you ever thought of using your TV as a stimulus to develop thinking and communication skills? Many parents unfortunately use the TV as a baby-sitter or a pacifier, but there is a better use for it. Consider the commercials. These too can be used to develop better communication and also perhaps lessen their manipulative hold upon the mind of a child. James White suggested a way to deal with commercials:

There's no way that you can force your children to hide their eyes and cover their ears when the television commercials appear. Those ads will always be there on the commercial stations. Keep in mind that our American system of commercial television networks requires the participation of advertisers who are willing to buy TV time in order to keep the stations' programs on the air. Rather than trying to avoid the TV pitches, you may find these questions useful in discussing the commercial messages.

1. Who's talking? Real, unpaid people? Or professional actors?

2. Who wrote the words that the people say?

3. Who's paying to put this commercial on TV? Why?

4. Is this commercial "live," or has it been filmed in scenes until the most desirable scene is used?

5. Would you ever expect to see a dog that didn't like the dog food? Why not?

6. How many breakfast foods can you name that you've seen on TV this week? How many breakfasts can you eat in a week? Then why are so many breakfast foods advertised?

Another way, more subtle and more interesting for older children, to get them aware of the "rigged world" of the family in the TV ads is to ask them if that's the way things are in real life, always will be, or should be. Do the TV ads show us real people in a real world? Do fathers wander through real bathrooms murmuring the name of a beloved mouthwash? Do children in real homes generally get stripped to the buff in front of the automatic washers? It seems that only boys in TV ads get dirty—don't the girls get dirty too? Perhaps you've noticed that only baby girls get their diapers changed in TV ads. Why? Perhaps baby boys don't soil their diapers! Do only women buy laundry detergent and wash dishes? Do white tornadoes really go whistling though kitchen windows? When's the last time you saw a covered wagon and horses disappear under the sink?

If you've discussed bossy sentences before now, you might ask the child to identify commands in commercials: "Buy three and save!" "Send for your free copy today!" "Compare, if you care!" With discussions and practice, you and the child will be able to determine commands, requests couched in questions and softened with courtesy words, and the more subtle directives—but this is not an overnight accomplishment.[4]

References

1. Lee Salk and Rita Kramer, *How to Raise a Human Being* (New York: Warner Books, 1973), pp. 115-16.
2. Silas L. Warner, M.D., and Edward Rosenberg, *Your Child Learns Naturally: What Can You Do to Help Prepare Your Child for School* (New York: Doubleday & Co., 1976), pp. 134-35.
3. Material in this section is adapted from Terrel H. Bell, *Active Parent Concern* (Englewood Cliffs: Prentice-Hall, 1976), pp. 49-50.
4. James D. White, *Talking with a Child* (New York: Macmillan Co., 1976), pp. 102-3.

6

Family Communication Patterns

Communication within the family environment is different from communication outside the home. It is helpful to understand the differences and their effect on the family.

Outside the home social customs dictate topics and appropriate times and places for conversation. In the home there is more freedom and flexibility. Usually there are no set times when family members talk about particular or assigned topics. Most families do not have regular times for problem-solving, decision-making, family administrative matters, pleasant and fun talk, or discovering what family members have been doing.

This unique characteristic of a less structured pattern of family communication has its advantages but may also be a medium for the growth of problems. Mealtime, for example, can become the time for handling family squabbles. Watching television can be the time for discussing schoolwork. Driving to church may be the time when family rules or discipline are covered each week. In most families certain kinds of family communication occur regularly with certain behaviors. What are some of these? Driving in the car, eating, getting dressed, watching television, getting dinner ready, washing the dishes. It appears then that these activities are somewhat controlling interchange. The nonverbal aspect of communication which is so important may be ignored because Mom or Dad is not looking at the other person who is talking or supposed to be listening.

If the behavior that the person is engaged in at the time he is communicating about something else is irritating or frustrating, this irritation could enter into the speaker's tone of voice, which then distorts the message he is conveying. And if most of the family arguments begin to occur during the dinner hour, the dinnertime begins to be the stimulus for family arguments. It's almost as though people are thinking, "Well, here comes the so-called happy dinnertime. What will we fight about tonight?"

Another characteristic of family communication involves the size of the communication audience. With a smaller number of people involved in the communication process, an individual is affected more by the behavior of the other persons. For example, if your spouse is a nonresponsive listener, he can limit your conversation as you begin to get discouraged. If your spouse is a good active listener, he can actually stimulate your conversation, which could develop into a problem of overtalking.

Because most families receive little corrective help for or evaluation of their communication patterns from people outside the family, faulty or poor patterns of communication may develop over the years. One such pattern that develops in many families is a transference of frustrations acquired during the day at work, school, or home by one family member to the others. If Dad has a bad day at work he may bring his troubles home and upset the rest of the family. If the kids have a poor day at school they may come home angry or dejected and say something that incites an argument.

Parents are basically alike, in that we bring with us to the family relationship models and patterns that we have seen or learned in the homes of our parents. Some are healthy and some are not. Here are several types of responses that tend to hamper communication between parents and children.

The Critic is sarcastic and is guilty of ridiculing, name-calling, and inappropriate joking. The critic makes statements such as:

"You're a lazy child."

"You just think you're a smarty pants, don't you?"

"Oh, look at Mr. Big Shot."

"Don't tell me your teacher is too hard. You just need to apply yourself. I don't blame her for getting upset. If I were in a room with a bunch of wild kids I'd get like that too."

The Scriptures warn against criticism and suggest alternate behavior:

"Let us therefore stop turning critical eyes on one another. Let us rather be critical of our own conduct and see that we do nothing to make a brother stumble or fall" (Rom. 14:13, PH).

"Fathers, do not provoke or irritate or fret your children —do not be hard on them or harass them; lest they become discouraged and sullen and morose and feel inferior and frustrated; do not break their spirit" (Col. 3:21, AMP).

"As a madman who casts firebrands, arrows, and death, so is the man who deceives his neighbor and then says, 'Was I not joking?' " (Prov. 26:18-19, AMP)

Peter Psychiatrist is a diagnostician, an analyzer, and an interrogator. He says:

"I know what your problem is . . . "

"Okay, tell me what happened so I can figure out how to solve it for you."

"How long have you felt angry at your teacher? Why do you feel that way? Who else knows about how you feel?"

The Judge does a lot of evaluating and makes a lot of pronouncements.

"I think you got what was coming to you."

"Well, you asked for it and you got it."

"You didn't study as hard as you could. That's why . . ."

"If you had spent more time practicing you wouldn't have . . ."

"All of you are wrong on that subject. Why didn't you read more?"

The Know-It-All has the final word on everything. He shows himself as being superior, and he lectures, preaches and advises.

"I've had much more experience than you have . . ."

"Listen to me—I'm older and I've gone to school for . . ."

"That just doesn't mean anything. There's no sense to it. Now listen to me . . ."

"I wouldn't do that if I were you. Here's the right way to do it."

"Oh come on. You know better. How many times do I have to tell you? Don't you have a brain?"

The Commander-in-Chief may feel that Ephesians 5 gives him the power and the right to act in a dictatorial manner. Too often a person operating in this manner is really insecure, impatient, and easily threatened within himself. He responds with orders, commands, threats, and other means of controlling.

"I told you, get to it now!"

"Do it now. I don't want to hear what you are saying. Now move!"

"You're going to do as I say. I've made up my mind."

"I don't want you to talk to me or your mother like that; and quit your crying."

How Do You Talk?

How do you talk? How does your family talk? How do your spouse and your children talk? Ask yourself these questions. Better yet, write down your initial response. You will learn much about your family.

1. How do your family members talk to you?
2. Describe how they talk to one another.
3. How does what you say affect what they say?

4. How does what they say affect what you talk about?
5. Which member of your family talks the least?
6. Which member of your family talks the most?
7. Which member talks first?
8. Which member talks last?
9. Which member doesn't talk unless asked to talk?
10. Which member tends to attack what others say?
11. Which member uses the harshest words?
12. Which member asks the most questions?
13. Which member talks more about facts?
14. Which member talks most about feelings?
15. Which member does not talk on a feeling level?

When you have finished answering these questions, ask each of the other family members to answer them and then discuss your responses. In doing this you may learn not only what they believe and think but also why. The discoveries that you make might be surprising and lead to additional questions such as, Who dominates the conversation? You will discover the answer from looking at all of the answers to one question and not just your own answers. You may feel that your oldest child does most of the talking, but what if everyone else thinks it is you? Why does one person talk so much? Is it from insecurity? Why is it that one doesn't talk very much? Is he shy or timid or lazy? Does he know that it irritates others? Is everyone given an equal opportunity to talk or is it a contest? What kind of talk is going on? Negative or positive? Simple or complex? Factual or emotional?

Building a Relationship for Communication

Communication does not just happen. Of course there are times when we formally structure a communication time or experience, but the best times of communication occur naturally and spontaneously. What happens to bring this type of a family atmosphere about? Let me make some suggestions which will build a relationship that enhances the communication process.

1. What are your attitudes toward your children? Trying to build positive communication with underlying negative attitudes just will not work. Our feelings affect our attitudes and actions toward our children. Here are some suggested possibilities:

If I Feel This Way	*I Might Act Like This*
Children are to be seen and not heard.	I ignore my four-year-old while talking to a friend in the store.
Children don't know very much.	I'm impatient when he doesn't get his spelling right.
A child is a nuisance to be endured.	I call him clumsy when he spills his milk.
My work is more important than playing with him.	I give excuses about having work to do when he wants to play. I also make him feel guilty for asking by saying my work is more important.
I work hard and don't want to be bothered when I get home.	I pretend that I'm listening when he comes up to talk to me.
A child can't think for himself.	I say, "You're too little to choose."
My friends will judge me for the way my child acts.	I usually don't take him with me. If I do, I threaten him with what will happen if he doesn't sit still and behave himself.

| Men should not show emotions. That's for women. | I don't kiss or hug my child nor do I share my feelings with him. |

These are just a few possibilities. You may know of some others. If we have a child who wasn't planned for or if we have all girls and no boys (but really wanted boys), what is our attitude? What if our child has a handicap or is deformed? What if the last child was born in our early forties when we were looking forward to freedom from children? Even if we are not totally aware of our own attitudes, children are. They can see through us and they pick up messages from us. If we say that we want to sit down and communicate but they know differently, we may not get the response that we were looking for. The words of Jesus speak to us as parents: "[The] mouth speaks from that which fills his heart" (Luke 6:45, NASB).

2. What are our priorities? If our spouse and children are not near the top of our list of priorities, then they will suffer. Can you identify a specific time each day when you are able to relate to each of your children in a personal, meaningful manner? Think of one time for each of the past seven days.

3. Maintain quality time instead of quantity. What do you do together that your child enjoys? Do you shop together? Study together? Look at bugs together? Take your child to work with you so he can know more about your world? Have you ever gone for an entire month without turning on the TV and used that time to talk, play games, or share together? When time is used up it is gone forever and there is no second chance.

4. Learn to listen with your eyes. Our eyes pick up the nonverbal part of communication. When your child comes in slouching and walking slowly and you ask "What's wrong?" and he says "Nothing," do you let it go at that or do you make yourself available to him and continue to draw him out, knowing that by the way he is walking and looking

he appears to have something on his mind? What does it mean when you go into a new store and your child takes your hand in his? What does it mean when your child says he wants to sit next to you? If Father is going away on a trip what kind of nonverbal cues does your child give that reflect his feelings? [1]

Paul Welter offered some additional suggestions:

1. Do not hurry another member of your family unnecessarily. The time gained is not worth the price of a relationship.

2. Treat the members of your family with courtesy.

3. Get the dialogue going.

4. Rebuild the relationship when necessary. [2]

References

1. Suggestions adapted from Norman Wakefield, *You Can Have a Happier Family* (Glendale, Calif.: Gospel Light Publications, 1975), chapter 5.
2. Paul Welter, *Family Problems and Predicaments* (Wheaton: Tyndale House, 1977), pp. 131-33.

7

The Gift of Listening

Many of the finest gifts that a child receives as he is growing up are intangible. One of these gifts, not only for a child but for all people, is the gift of listening. Paul Tournier said, "How beautiful, how grand and liberating this experience is, when people learn to help each other. It is impossible to overemphasize the immense need humans have to be really listened to. Listen to all the conversations of our world, between nations as well as those between couples. They are, for the most part, dialogues of the deaf." [1]

At one time I heard a speaker make this statement: "We hear only half of what is said to us, understand only half of that, believe only half of that, and remember only half of that!" If this is true, we're in trouble!

When you and I listen to another person we are conveying the thought that "I'm interested in you as a person, and I think that what you feel is important. I respect your thoughts, even if I don't agree with them. I know that they are valid for you. I feel sure that you have a contribution to make. I'm not trying to change you or evaluate you. I just want to understand you. I think you're worth listening to, and I want you to know that I'm the kind of person that you can talk to." [2]

God Listens

Have you had this experience of being really listened to? Has your child experienced this? The model for being real listeners is found in the Word of God.

The eyes of the Lord are toward the righteous,
And His ears are open to their cry.
The face of the Lord is against evildoers,
To cut off the memory of them from the earth.
The righteous cry and the Lord hears,
And delivers them out of all their troubles.
The Lord is near to the brokenhearted,
And saves those who are crushed in spirit (Ps. 34:15-18, NASB).

I love the Lord, because He hears
my voice and my supplications.
Because He has inclined His ear to me,
Therefore I shall call upon Him as long as I live
(Ps. 116:1-2, NASB).

Call to Me, and I will answer you, and I will tell you great and mighty things, which you do not know (Jer. 33:3, NASB).

The Word of God also gives us directives concerning how *we* are to listen:

He who gives an answer before he hears,
It is folly and shame to him (Prov. 18:13, NASB).

Any story sounds true until someone tells the other side and sets the record straight (Prov. 18:17, LB).

The wise man learns by listening; the simpleton can learn only by seeing scorners punished (Prov. 21:11, LB).

. . . Let every man be quick to hear (a ready listener) (James 1:19, AMP).

What Is Listening?

What do we mean by listening? What do we mean by hearing? Is there a difference? Yes there is! Hearing is basically to gain content or information for your own purposes. Listening is caring for and being empathic toward another person. Hearing means that you are concerned about what is going on inside you during the conversation. Listening means you are trying to understand the feelings of the other person and are listening for his sake.

Let me give you a threefold definition of listening. (1) Listening means that when your child is talking to you, you are not thinking about what you are going to say when he stops talking. You are not busy formulating your response. You are concentrating on what is being said and are putting into practice Proverbs 18:13. (2) The second part of listening is complete acceptance without judgment of what is said or how it is said. You may fail to hear the message because you don't like the child's tone of voice or the words he has used. You may react on the spot to the tone and content and miss the meaning. Perhaps he hasn't said it in the best way, but why not listen and then come back later when both of you are calm, and discuss the proper wording and tone of voice? Acceptance does not mean you have to agree with the content of what is said. Rather, it means that you understand that what your child is saying is something he feels. (3) You should be able to repeat what your child has said and what you thought he was feeling when he was speaking to you. Real listening implies an obvious interest in the child's feelings and opinions and an attempt to understand them from his perspective.

Focused Attention

To be a listener and accomplish the three parts of this definition means that you must give your undivided attention to your child. Dr. Ross Campbell calls this "focused attention":

Eye contact and physical contact seldom require real sacrifice by parents. Focused attention does, however, require time, and sometimes a lot of it. It may mean giving up something parents would rather do. Loving parents will see times when a child desperately needs focused attention at a time when the parents feel least like giving it.

What is focused attention? Focused attention is giving a child our full, undivided attention in such a way that he feels without doubt that he is completely loved. That he is valuable enough *in his own right* to warrant parents' undistracted watchfulness, appreciation, and uncompromising regard. In short, focused attention makes a child feel he is the most important person in the world in his parents' eyes.

Some may think this is going a bit too far, but take a look at Scripture and see how highly children are regarded. Notice the high priority Christ gave them (Mark 10:13-16). Their value is stressed in the Psalms (127:3-5), and in Genesis, children are referred to as gifts (33:5)."[3]

Undivided Attention

Sometimes you may have to take it on yourself to get the other person's attention in order to have him listen to you. When our daughter was about six, she came home from school after an exciting day. I was reading the paper and she came up next to me and started to tell me what was so exciting. But I kept on reading the paper. About every ten seconds I'd say, "Mmm hmm, fine, yes," while she was telling her story, but I wasn't listening. All of a sudden there was dead silence—not a word. She stopped talking. A few seconds later a little hand came right down in the middle of my newspaper and pressed it down. I looked up and about a foot from my face there she was looking at me eyeball to eyeball. When she had my attention, she began again at the beginning of her story and told me once again every detail. She knew she had to have my attention first.

Sometimes we think we are giving other people our undivided attention, but we are not giving them sufficient time. I travel during the year, and I may, during the course of a year, take fifteen or twenty trips to different parts of the country for seminars. I usually arrive home on a Saturday night quite tired. But the family hasn't seen me for a couple of days and they like to talk.

I returned home one night and discovered that Joyce had taken our daughter out to get a new coat. We had promised her one and while I was gone, she bought it. As soon as my car pulled into the driveway, my daughter was out the door with her new coat on. She said, "Daddy, look at my new coat! Isn't it neat? Isn't it great?" I looked at it for a few seconds and said, "Yes, that really looks fine, Sheryl."

We got inside the house, finally, and she whirled around in her new coat again and said, "Daddy, do you like the coat? How does it look?" "It looks fine, Sheryl," and I walked off to the other room. About an hour later we were all sitting together in the family room talking and Sheryl turned and said in a quiet voice, "Daddy, even though you didn't look at my coat a long time, do you really like it?" We might think the amount of time that we spend is sufficient for the other person, but maybe it isn't.[4]

Results of Focused Attention

Focused attention is just another part of listening but it does have important results in the life of a child.

What is it that defines focused attention? When a child feels, "I'm all alone with my mommy (or daddy)"; "I have her (him) all to myself"; "at this moment, I'm the most important person in the world to my mother (father)"; this is the goal of focused attention, to enable a child to feel this way.

Focused attention is not something that is nice to give our child if time permits; it is a critical *need* each child has. How a child views himself and how he is accepted by his world is determined by the way in which this need is met. Without focused attention, a child experiences increased anxiety because he feels everything else is more important than he. A child is consequently less secure and is impaired in his emotional and psychological growth. Such a child can be identified in the nursery or classroom. He is less mature than children whose parents have taken the time to fill their need for focused attention. This unfortunate child is generally more withdrawn and has difficulty with peers. He is less able to cope and usually reacts poorly in any conflict. He is overly dependent upon the teacher or other adults he comes into contact with.

Some children, especially girls deprived of focused attention from their fathers, *seem* to be just the opposite. They are quite talkative, manipulative, dramatic, often childishly seductive, and are usually considered precocious, outgoing, and mature by their kindergarten and first grade teachers. However, as they grow older, this behavior pattern does not change and becomes gradually inappropriate. By the time they are in the third or fourth grade they are usually obnoxious to their peers, and to their teachers. However, even at this late date, focused attention, especially from the fathers, can go a long way in reducing the children's self-defeating behavior, decreasing their anxiety, and freeing them to resume their maturational growth.[5]

Be a Better Listener

How can you listen better? Consider these guidelines.

1. What you feel about your child and how you view your child affects how you listen to him. A child's communication is colored by how you view him. This view may have been shaped by your observations of his past performance or by your own defensiveness. Do you see your child as a complainer, whiner, bully, procrastinator, etc.? If so, how does this affect what you think you hear?

2. Remember that physiologically you can listen five times

as fast as you can speak. If your child talks at 100 words per minute and you can listen at 500 words per minute, what do you do with all of that extra time? Often boredom sneaks in and you daydream. If you have heard the story before, you put your ears on automatic pilot. Another problem is that of narrowness—hearing only what one wants to hear or agree with. This is seen when a child comes back later and says, "Mommy, I told you about that." And you say, "Oh no you didn't. I know—I was listening to you and you did not mention that." And yet if you could hear a tape recording of the conversation, you would realize that your child did tell you, but for some reason you blocked out what was said.

3. Listen with your ears, your eyes, and your body. If your child asks, "Are you listening to me?" and you say "Yes" while walking away or fixing dinner or doing the dishes, perhaps you aren't really listening. Concentrate on the person and the message, giving your undivided attention. Turn off the appliance or TV when there is an important matter to talk about; set aside what you are doing and listen.

There are several responses that you could make to indicate to your child that you are listening and catching all of what he is saying. *Clarifying* is one of these responses. This response reflects on your child's meaning and the intention of what he has said. "I think what you're saying is that you trust me to keep my promise to you, but you are still a bit concerned about my being away just before your birthday."

Observing is another skill. This response focuses upon the nonverbal or tonal quality of what your child has said. "I noticed that your voice was dropping when you talked about the test results."

Another well-known response is called *reflective listening*. A reflective statement attempts to pick up the feelings expressed by the child. Usually a feeling word is included in the response, such as, "You seem quite sad (joyful, happy, delighted, angry, etc.) about that."

Inquiring is yet another helpful response. An inquiry

draws out more information about the meaning of what was said. A very simple response would be, "I would like you to tell me more if you can."

4. Be patient, especially if your child is a slow or a hesitant talker. You may have a tendency to jump in whenever you can find an opening, finish a statement for the child, or hurry him up. You cannot assume that you really know what is going to be said. You cannot read your child's mind.

James White has given a helpful definition and examples of listening to small children, which can help you build relationships. He describes what to do when you first sit down with a child to play with him:

At first, play a private game with yourself. When you decide to join the child, promise yourself that you *won't* say the first word after you sit down. If you're ignored for a few moments, fret not. That only gives you more time to observe the action and to enjoy the child's reaction. If you get a smile, smile back. But bite your tongue till you can't stand the pain; keeping quiet may help you to get into the child's interest instead of changing the scene with your own vocal entrance. If the child is molding something with modeling clay, you might start your own clay figure. Perhaps the child asks, "What do you want?" You can say, "I want to be with you awhile and to do what you do," or make some other cordial reply that indicates you're interested in the child's activity. But, whatever the opening, see if you can wait long enough for the child to speak first, giving you a cue on where to go from there.

Active listening means more than muttering a repertoire of senseless bromides during the pauses in another person's talk. You're losing quite steadily when you use almost exclusively a stream of conversation killers such as these with a child: "Huh-uh . . . That's nice . . . Too bad . . . Oh . . . Uh-huh . . . Hm-m-m . . . Well . . . I see . . ." There are moments in a conversation when you're expected to nod your head, smile, or frown slightly, or make some noise to indicate that you're awake and comprehending. But these words, and nothing more on your side of the talk, tend to place an increasingly heavy burden on the young child, who runs out of verbal gas for lack of substantial responses from you.

Active listening means that you steer the young speaker with comments and questions that encourage him to continue talking. . . .

You must hear the child's story and attempt to follow the sequence. If you can, comment or question in order to get the events straight in your own mind. . . .[6]

References

1. Paul Tournier, *To Understand Each Other* (Atlanta: John Knox Press, 1967), p. 29.
2. George E. and Nikki Koehler, *My Family: How Shall I Live with It?* (Chicago: Rand McNally & Co., 1968), p. 57.
3. D. Ross Campbell, *How to Really Love Your Child* (Wheaton: Victor Books, 1977), p. 55.
4. Norman Wright, *An Answer to Family Communication* (Irvine, Calif.: Harvest House, 1977), pp. 56-58.
5. Campbell, pp. 60-61.
6. James White, *Talking with a Child* (New York: Macmillan Co., 1976), pp. 16-17.

8

Are You a Positive or a
Negative Communicator?

How would your family members describe your communication patterns? If they had to say whether your conversation is basically positive or negative, which would it be? Perhaps there would be a difference between their answer and what you would like them to say. Let's look at what our communication should not be, and then at what it should be.

"Many Christian homes today are citadels oı criticism. Words that tear down a person do not correct a problem but usually intensify it and help to lower the self-esteem of the other person. Typical comments are, 'Anyone could have done that. It's not so special.' 'You may not be pretty but beauty isn't everything.' 'How can you be so stupid? A two-year-old could have done better.' When you engage in attributing insulting characteristics to another person, you are engaging in a process called character assassination.

"How does your response affect family members? Are they helped by the statements? Does your message give them insight into what they may have done that was wrong? Will they be able to do a better job next time? Telling a person that he is stupid or dumb for his lack of ability to pound a nail straight doesn't teach him to hammer it correctly. Yelling at one's wife for her being late or telling friends about it in her presence doesn't help her to be on time." [1]

The Word of God has an answer for this: "Stop turning critical eyes on one another. Let us rather be critical of our own conduct and see that we do nothing to make a brother stumble or fall" (Rom. 14:13, PH). The Scripture also tells us to "encourage one another" (1 Thes. 5:14).

Faultfinding

Sven Wahlroos wrote that "criticism must be discriminate and take into account the fact that no human being is perfect and that there are many matters which are so unimportant that they should be ignored. . . . When criticism becomes indiscriminate it is called faultfinding and it leads to most destructive consequences.

"[These] are the factors which make faultfinding so destructive:

1. Faultfinding is destructive because of its very definition. It is defined here in terms of communications as a way of saying: "I do not accept you as a human being because I will not recognize in practice and in daily living that human beings are imperfect." In other words, faultfinding expresses a lack of acceptance of people and a distorted view of reality.

2. Because of the basic lack of acceptance involved, faultfinding ruins human relationships, makes people feel hostile toward each other, sours the daily atmosphere of the home, and makes it a place of misery rather than of happiness and satisfaction.

3. Faultfinding is destructive not only to the "victims" (many of whom are not as innocent as it may appear), but to the faultfinder himself or herself, as well. That is because faultfinding makes the other person either turn you off completely, counterattack or store up resentment against you. . . .

4. It follows that faultfinding is an ineffective method

for changing the behavior of others. It may produce initial results, but if it is kept up it will lead to the other person not really hearing what you are saying; he may hear it in a mechanical sense but it will soon 'go out through the other ear.' Rest assured, however, that the lack of acceptance involved is received and understood.

5. Thus, faultfinding can be dangerous because when the time comes that you have a truly necessary and important criticism to make, you are powerless then, having diluted the effectiveness of your arguments in advance so that they no longer mean anything to the person being criticized. The danger is especially apparent in the case of children who—through faultfinding—have been taught to think: 'Never mind, it's just that cranky old parent-faultfinder putting on his broken record again.'

6. Faultfinding teaches unreasonableness and intolerance. Since it induces distaste, it may lead the other party (spouse, child, employee, etc.) to become unreasonable in the other extreme by becoming especially careless and making an excessive number of mistakes, thus setting up a neurotic interaction. . . .

7. Faultfinding is a consequence of reliance on certain destructive defense mechanisms. The typical faultfinder either projects his own shortcomings onto another person or displaces his anger toward one person (e.g. boss) onto another (e.g. wife). Most often, faultfinding is an unconscious way of trying to hide one's own weaknesses by projecting them onto someone else." [2]

Many parents have a tendency to focus on the mistakes of their children. If you do this, you are actually taking the child's attention away from positive ideas and thoughts and redirecting them toward the negative. When this is done you only reinforce the possibility that your child will repeat that negative behavior. In addition you could create such a fear of making a mistake that you actually set him up to make more mistakes. When your child has done something wrong or has made a mistake, it is much more important to place an emphasis on what you want him to do in the future; focus on what he has done correctly rather than magnify the mistakes.

Your child needs encouragement. He probably needs encouragement as much as demonstrations of love. A lack of encouragement could be considered a major cause for mistakes and for misbehavior. Encouragement is a continual process in which you give your child a sense of self-respect and also a sense of accomplishment.

What can be done or what can be said when correction becomes necessary? You can't go around all the time without offering some suggestions or corrections, can you?

Guidelines for Communication

Here are some guidelines for praise, criticism, and complaints.

1. Any communication that you share with your family members should show regard for the other person's worth as a human being created in the image of God; he is either now or potentially a joint heir with Christ. Your communication should also encourage his own personal development and give that person motivation and self-confidence.

2. Your praise-to-criticism ratio should be about 80 or 90 percent praise to 20 or 10 percent criticism. In many families this ratio unfortunately is just the opposite.

3. Do you look for improvement in the other person or have you labeled your child as bad or negative or lacking? Do you allow for improvement or change and reinforce it when it occurs? It's easy to find mistakes and negative elements in a person's behavior, but it is just as easy to find desirable and positive elements if you look for them. It also helps to use a child's past performance as a yardstick. Praise and encouragement can be based on improvements and not on total attainment on the present standard.

4. When your child does make a mistake or fails in some accomplishment, it is important to avoid any word or actions

that indicate that you consider *him* a failure. You can separate the deed from the doer. A person can lack in skill or knowledge but that does not lessen his value as a person.

5. Consider your expectations for your children. Are they realistic and attainable? Do you accept your children as children? Consider what Dr. Ross Campbell has said concerning unconditional love:

How I wish I could say, "I love my children all the time regardless of anything else, including their behavior." But like all parents, I cannot, yet I will give myself credit for trying to arrive at that wonderful goal of loving them unconditionally. I do this by constantly reminding myself that:

a. they are children

b. they will tend to act like children

c. much of childish behavior is unpleasant

d. if I do my part as a parent and love them despite their childish behavior, they will be able to mature and give up childish ways

e. if I only love them when they please me (conditional love), and convey my love to them only during those times, they will not feel genuinely loved. This in turn will make them insecure, damage their self-image, and actually prevent them from moving on to better self-control and more mature behavior. Therefore, their behavior and its development is *my* responsibility as much as theirs

f. if I love them unconditionally, they will feel good about themselves and be comfortable with themselves. They will then be able to control their anxiety and, in turn, their behavior, as they grow into adulthood

g. if I only love them when they meet my requirements or expectations, they will feel incompetent. They will be-believe it is fruitless to do their best because it is never enough. Insecurity, anxiety, and low self-esteem will plague them. They will be constant hindrances in their emotional and behavioral growth. Again, their total growth is as much my responsibility as theirs

    h. for my sake as a struggling parent, and for my sons' (and daughters') sakes, I pray my love for my children will be as unconditional as I can make it. The future of my children depends on this foundation.[3]

6. When you do have a valid criticism or complaint to make, make it specific and positive. Most complaints or gripes are too general and negative. "You kids are so messy!" "You never show me any consideration." "You never put your things away." "Don't you be mean to your brother while I'm gone." Most of these statements are calling attention to the problem or negative behavior. It would be far better to make these complaints specific and positive, pointing toward the desired behavior. For example, "I would appreciate it if you would hang up your coat and put your books on the chair." "When I say that I'm not feeling well, I would appreciate it if you would fix yourself a snack and play quietly by yourself for an hour."

Encourage or Discourage?

The authors of *Raising a Responsible Child* have given a helpful outline distinguishing between words that encourage and words that discourage.[4]

Words that encourage	Words that discourage
Knowing you, I'm sure that you will do fine.	Knowing you, I think that you should do more.
You can make it.	You usually make mistakes so be careful.
I have faith in you.	I doubt that you can do it.
Thanks for your help.	If you had finished clearing the table, that would have been helpful.

You're doing fine.	You can do better.
I enjoyed that song.	Your music is getting better, but you missed the notes at the end.
I can see you put a lot of effort into that.	That is a good job, but the corners are ragged.
You have really improved.	Well, you're playing a little better than last year.
You'll figure it out.	You had better get some help. That looks very difficult.
You can only learn by trying.	I doubt you should try.
That was a good effort. Don't worry about the mistake.	Why didn't you think of that before you started?
Let's think this through together.	How can you be so dumb?
You've done some good thinking. Are you ready to start?	That plan will never work.
That's a challenge. But I'm sure you'll make it.	That is too difficult for you. I'll do it.

You may want to take some time to think about and then write down some of the complaints and gripes that you have with your own children. Rephrase these into positive and specific statements. Whenever you do share a concern such as this, it might help for a while to ask your child what he heard you saying and to repeat it to you to make sure that your statement registered.

References

1. Norman Wright, *An Answer to Family Communication* (Irvine, Calif.: Harvest House, 1977), pp. 17-18.
2. Sven Wahlroos, *Family Communication* (New York: Macmillan Co., 1974), pp. 20-21.
3. D. Ross Campbell, M.D., *How to Really Love Your Children* (Wheaton: Victor Books, 1977), pp. 30-31.
4. Don Dinkmeyer and Gary McKay, *Raising a Responsible Child* (New York: Simon & Schuster, 1973), pp. 99-101.

9

Are You an Emotional or a
Factual Communicator?

What do you talk about and how do you talk? What does the word *sharing* mean to you? Have you thought of sharing as different than talking? Sharing is a form of talking but it involves opening up and giving yourself as you talk. It's the type of communication that will let other people really get to know you. It's the type of communication that lets you really know your child. Sharing involves giving your thoughts, feelings, ideas, and experiences to others. Actually what it involves is you taking the initiative to reveal something of yourself that is important to you. When you share your feelings, thoughts, and ideas with your child, you will create a closer relationship as you become more real to him. You lower the likelihood of being so remote and threatening that he cannot approach you. And your child will also share.

What have you shared lately with your child? For many years as our daughter was growing up she asked, "Tell me about when you were a little boy, Daddy," and I would. That question caused me to think and to remember, and it brought back many feelings as well. It was a good question and it gave my daughter a better picture of me. I also discovered something else. I found that my daughter would compare her present world with my past world and thus it became a learning experience for her. It helps a child identify with you as he begins to understand that you had feelings and situations and problems just like he does.

In many families the communication exists on a very superficial level. Clichés and trite phrases are used excessively. Talking about school, work, the weather, sports, and safe activities are the main content of the family's communication. The same questions, statements, and content are repeated day after day after day! No one really gets to know the others on a deep level because they don't talk about their own ideas, opinions, or feelings.

Emotional vs. Factual Communication

Let's compare emotional communication with factual communication. Dr. Ross Campbell has described these two patterns:

We can start by realizing that there is a difference between cognitive (that is, intellectual or rational) communications and emotional (that is, feeling) communications. Persons who communicate primarily on a cognitive level deal mainly with factual data. They like to talk about such topics as sports, the stock market, money, houses, jobs, etc., keeping the subject of conversation out of the emotional area. Usually they are quite uncomfortable dealing with issues which elicit feelings, especially unpleasant feelings such as anger. Consequently, they avoid talking about subjects which involve love, fear, and anger. These persons have difficulty, then, being warm and supportive of their spouses.

Others communicate more on the feeling level. They tire easily of purely factual data, and feel a need to share feelings, especially with their spouses. They feel the atmosphere between husband and wife must be as free as possible from unpleasant feelings like tension, anger, and resentment. So, of course, they want to talk about these emotional things, resolve conflicts with their spouse, clear the air, and keep things pleasant between them.

Of course no one is completely cognitive or completely emotional.[1]

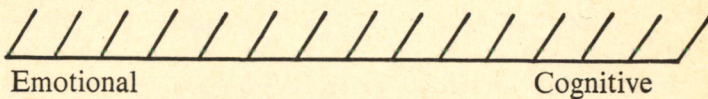

Emotional   Cognitive

1. Indicate where you are on this graph by placing your initials near the appropriate mark.

2. Indicate where each of your family members is on the chart, using their initials.

3. Indicate where you think they would place you on the chart. Mark your initials and circle them. . . .

A person on the left side of the graph, who shares more feelings, is not less bright or less intellectual. This person is simply aware of his/her feelings and is usually better able to do something about them. On the other hand, a person on the right side of the graph, who displays less feelings, does not *have* less feelings; the feelings are simply suppressed and buried, and this person is less aware and often blind to his feelings.

A surprising fact is that the so-called cognitive person (on the right) is controlled by his feelings just as is the so-called emotional person but *he doesn't realize it.* For example, the stiff, formal intellectual has deep feelings also, but uses enormous energy to keep them buried so he won't be bothered with them. But unfortunately they *do* bother him. Whenever someone (like an "emotional" wife, or child) is around asking him for affection and warmth, he is not only unable to respond, he is angered that his precious equilibrium has been disturbed.[2]

Childhood Sensitivity

Where do you think we find most children on the graph?

Way over on the left side. A child comes into the world

with an amazing ability to perceive emotionally. The child is so sensitive to the feelings of his mother. It is a beautiful thing to see a newborn infant brought to his mother for the first time, if the mother truly wants him. He conforms to the mother's body and his contentment is obvious to all. . . .

It is very important to realize that from birth, children are extremely sensitive emotionally. Since their fund of knowledge is of course small, their way of communicating with their world is primarily on the feeling level. This is crucial. Do you see it? A child's first impressions of the world are through his feelings. This is wonderful yet frightening when we think of the importance of it. A child's emotional being determines how he sees his world —his parents, his home, himself.

This sets the stage and foundation for almost everything else. For example, if a child sees his world as rejecting, unloving, uncaring, hostile, then what I consider a child's greatest enemy—anxiety—will be harmful to his speech, behavior, ability to relate and to learn. The point is that a child is not only emotionally supersensitive but also vulnerable.[3]

The Power of Words

Communication is made up of messages. Words are part of communication and they are important.

Children attending school soon learn to chant the sing-song poem, "Sticks and stones may break my bones, but words will never hurt me." But experience quickly teaches that this is untrue. Words can and do hurt a person. The Bible recognizes this and talks about word power in both the Old and New Testaments.

Proverbs 18:21 states what many have discovered: "Death and life are in the power of the tongue" (NASB). Proverbs 26:22 also speaks of how words really get to a person: "The words of a whisperer . . . go down to the innermost parts of the body" (NASB). This was what Job was experiencing when he cried in frustration, "How long will you torment me, and crush me with words?" (NASB) or as The Living Bible puts it, "How long are you going to trouble me, and try to break me with your words?" (Job 19:2)

James 3:2-10 talks about the power of words and why it is so important to control the tongue. Surely here are key ideas for improving communications in a marriage:

"If anyone can control his tongue, it proves that he has perfect control over himself in every other way. We can make a large horse turn around and go wherever we want by means of a small bit in his mouth.

"And a tiny rudder makes a huge ship turn wherever the pilot wants it to go, even though the winds are strong.

"So the tongue is a small thing, but what enormous damage it can do. A great forest can be set on fire by one tiny spark. And the tongue is a flame of fire. It is full of wickedness, and poisons every part of the body. And the tongue is set on fire by hell itself, and can turn our whole lives into a blazing flame of destruction and disaster.

"Men have trained, or can train, every kind of animal or bird that lives and every kind of reptile and fish, but no human being can tame the tongue. It is always ready to pour out its deadly poison. Sometimes it praises our heavenly Father, and sometimes it breaks out into curses against men who are made like God. And so blessing and cursing come pouring out of the same mouth. Dear brothers, surely this is not right!" (LB)

James compares the power of the tongue to the rudder of a ship, as far as power is concerned. Comparatively speaking, a rudder is a small part of the ship, yet it can turn the ship in any direction and control its destiny. What husbands and wives say to one another can turn their marriage in different directions (and in some cases cause them to wind up going in a vicious circle).

Continuing to emphasize the tongue's potency, James compares it to a flame of fire. Great forests can be leveled by one tiny spark. In the same way, a marriage can be damaged and in some cases even "set on fire" by one remark, or (more typically) by continually chopping and snipping away at each other.[4]

Communication through words can be a powerful force for building up or tearing down. In our culture, communication by words has been stressed so much that many just respond to words and little else. We do rely on them but there are other important parts of our messages as well.

Nonverbal Communication

Our behavior, the nonverbal element of our communication, is probably our most revealing means of communicating. Our words can be distorted and deceptive but our nonverbal behavior is probably the purest form of communication that we have. Studies have been conducted to determine how we communicate. They reveal that our feelings are conveyed through our words, our tone of voice, and our nonverbal behavior. Our words in face-to-face communication with another person account for 7 percent of the message, our tone of voice accounts for 38 percent, and our nonverbal behavior 55 percent. Did you realize the effect of your tone of voice and your behavior? You could take one sentence and convey many different meanings simply by making changes in your tone of voice. Your behavior is telling the other person something as well. All three parts of this communication message should be consistent or we create confusion on the part of the listener. A full communicator is one whose mind and emotions are aware of what is being shared; his message is consistent.

If you say in an offhand way while you are busy doing some task, "Johnny, I love you," can he believe it? Does your behavior say that he is important and did your tone of voice say that as well? If a husband says to his wife with the proper tone of voice, "Honey, I love you," but has his head buried in a newspaper, what is she to believe? If a wife asks, "How was your day?" in a flat tone as she passes by her husband on the way to another room, what should he respond to? The verbal or the nonverbal message? What about the husband who, as he leaves for work, comes up to his wife, smiles, gives her a big hug and kiss, and says in a soft, loving voice, "I love you and I'll miss you today"? Should his wife believe the message? Of course. At least for the time being. But as she closes the door and walks through the house and notices a newspaper in the middle of the room, pajamas on the bed, dirty socks on the floor and the cap off the hairspray can and left in the sink, what is she to believe? For years she has shared with her husband how important it is to her for him to pick up after himself. He says that he loves her. But now she begins to doubt it, for if he really loved her wouldn't he have learned to be more considerate?

Tonal Communication

Have you listened to your tone of voice? Have you listened to your behavior? Most of us are very conscious of our words but we will learn more about ourselves and others when we listen to tone of voice and behavior. Dr. Mark Lee said, "Marital problems may grow out of unsatisfactory nonverbal communications. Vocal variables are important carriers of meaning. We interpret the sound of a voice, both consciously and subconsciously. We usually can tell the emotional meanings of the speaker by voice pitch, rate of speech, loudness, and voice quality. We can tell the sincerity or insincerity, the conviction or lack of conviction, the truth or falsity of most statements we hear. When a voice is raised in volume and pitch, the words will not convey the same meaning as when spoken softly in a lower register. The high loud volume, with rapid rate and harsh quality, will likely communicate a degree of emotion that will greatly obscure the verbal message. The nonverbal manner in which a message is delivered is registered most readily by the listener. It may or may not be remembered for recall. However, the communicator tends to recall what he said rather than the manner of his speech." [5]

Let's consider what some nonverbal or voice behaviors might mean. Look at the following list and try to give two or three meanings to each behavior.

1. A child nods his head up and down.
2. A person turns her head rapidly in a certain direction.
3. A person smiles slightly.
4. A person's lower lip quivers slightly.
5. A person speaks in a loud, harsh voice.
6. A person speaks in a low, monotonous voice.
7. A person suddenly opens his eyes wide.
8. A person keeps her eyes lowered as she speaks to you.
9. A person speaks in a very halting or hesitant voice.
10. A person yawns during a conversation.
11. A person shrugs his shoulders.
12. A person is sitting rigid and upright in her chair.
13. A person has his arms folded tightly across his chest.
14. A person wrings her hands.
15. A person holds his chair tightly with his hands.
16. A person's breathing is quite irregular.
17. A person starts to turn pale.
18. A person keeps fiddling with his shirt collar.
19. A person slouches in her chair.
20. A person is constantly squirming.
21. A person inhales quickly.
22. A person continuously moves her legs back and forth.
23. A person hits his forehead with his hand.

If you would like to know more about the nonverbal behaviors in your family, conduct the following experiment. Make a list of as many of your own nonverbal behaviors as you can think of. Ask each member of the family to do this. After you have made your list, indicate in writing what you think each behavior means to the other members of the family. After each member has done this for himself, begin to share what you have written about yourself. Ask each person what your nonverbal behavior actually means or conveys to them. You may be in for a surprise.

Consistency

How can you use this information about how we communicate in a positive manner with your children? Just becoming aware of these facts may help you to become a better communicator. If family members are made aware of the meaning and importance of nonverbal behavior, some of the contradictory messages that may have been occurring can be pointed out, discussed, and resolved. For example, if a child's parents keep telling him to put away his toys after playing with them, yet he sees Mom or Dad leaving their reading material or hobbies scattered all over the room, he is getting a contradictory message. He may just be following the model that he is seeing.

If your child appears tired because he is sulking and whining and is irritable, what happens when you suggest that he is tired and may need to take a rest? Most often a child states that he isn't tired and he doesn't "need any old rest!" But if you first of all clearly point out his behaviors which are conveying to you that he might be tired or not feeling well, you are letting him know that he is communicating something to you. If you have a child who insists upon staying up later than he should each night to watch TV and insists that it doesn't affect him (but in the morning he doesn't get up and when he does he is Charley Crab), instead of arguing with him point out his behavior. Dr. Sven Wahlroos gave a clear example of how to handle this.

Johnny says that he is old enough to stay up later at night and that he does not need so much sleep. However, it is almost impossible to get him up in the morning in time to go to school. In this example, many parents would say: "No Johnny, you are tired and you need your sleep; you can't stay up later." This is usually futile because Johnny does not feel tired and he thinks he is a better expert than you on the question of whether he is tired or not and on how much sleep he needs. And certainly some children do need less sleep than their parents think. So when you say that you know better than he whether he is tired and needs more sleep, he will see you as an unreasonable adult who either likes to show his power and push little kids around or wants to get his child out of the way, or perhaps both. His indignant resistance may lead to your nagging him every evening. It may lead to a lot of unpleasantness, fighting, and unhappiness.

However, if you recognize that you are being given contradictory messages and point this out, the child cannot feel that you are being unreasonable. He may still claim that you are not fair, but secretly he will know that your point is well taken. What you can say to him, then, is something like this: "Johnny, you make me confused! In the evening you tell me that you need less sleep, but in the morning you tell me that you need more sleep. Please MAKE UP YOUR MIND ABOUT WHAT YOU REALLY WANT AND THEN WE WILL DISCUSS IT AGAIN. If for two weeks you tell me both in the evening and in the morning that you need less sleep, then we will let you stay up half an hour longer." Johnny may well object to this arrangement and give you some "static" about it, but secretly he will know that it is fair and reasonable. Thus, you can listen to his objections to be sure that you have taken his ideas and feelings into account but if he cannot come up with a reasonable point in favor of his position, you must be firm and insist on being given the same message in the morning as in the evening.[6]

If you begin to practice this style of communicating, what will your reaction be if your child learns it and one day points out some contradictory behavior on your part? Will you be able to admit it, thank him for pointing it out, and change? After all, that's what we are asking *him* to do.

Total Listening

Earlier we talked about listening. Total listening means that we try to listen to all of the messages that are being sent, such as the nonverbal behavior, the tone of voice, and the words. Silence, for example, is nonverbal communication and may be conveying a message.

Listen to your child's face and body. Nonverbal behavior can confirm what a person is saying. If your child says that he agrees with you and he is nodding his head at the same time, his behavior is confirming what he is saying. Nonverbal behavior can also deny and confuse another person. If your child says to you that he is not upset and his upper lip is quivering, what will you believe? If you tell your child that you are angry and upset with him and you have a smile on your face, you might be confusing him.

Nonverbal behavior can strengthen or emphasize what is being said. If your child says that he doesn't want to come in the house and stamps his foot, his behavior is telling you something. If your child comes running up to you after having opened a gift and says "Thank-you" and throws his arms around you, the message is stronger.

Nonverbal behavior can add emotional color to the message. If a child says that a friend of his was mean to him and he puts his face in his hands when he is saying this, he is indicating how much he felt hurt. If you state in a firm voice that you are angry with your child and stalk out of the room, your behavior is definitely emphasizing your feelings.

Voice Quality

The quality of your voice or your child's voice will also be involved in the message. A harsh or soft tone can be very important to the total message. A few years ago we bought our first dog, which happened to be a sheltie. It is a very intelligent breed. The dog handler told me when I purchased Prince never to strike him but to train him with my tone of voice. When he told me that I had a few doubts, but I put it into practice. He was right. Just by changing the tonal quality of my voice I can send him straight to his bed or bring him running toward me. He responds beautifully to both tone of voice and nonverbal behaviors such as snapping the fingers or pointing at him to stop, or holding my palm up for him to stop, or flat down for him to lie down. He has also provided an element of conviction for me; on some occasions when I was speaking in a tone of voice to the other family members that I shouldn't have been using, all of a sudden I noticed Prince slinking away to his own bed. He thought I was scolding him!

Your voice quality can confirm what you are saying. If you tell your child you're upset with him and your voice is strained or quaking, your message is being confirmed. Your voice can also deny and confuse what is being said. If you ask Johnny if he would like to go to the store with you and he says in a slow voice, "Well, I guess so," his voice may be saying that he doesn't.

Your tone can strengthen or emphasize what you are saying. If you go into your child's room and say in a deliberate, firm voice, "Son, I'll give you two seconds to get out of that bed and I mean move right now!" he will get the message. And your tone can add emotional color to what you are saying. If you are apologizing to your child for something that you have done and your voice is slow, soft, and sensitive, the message is consistent.

When your child communicates with you, listen to the total message. Listen to the words, the behavior, the tone, and the context of the message.

References

1. D. Ross Campbell, M.D., *How to Really Love Your Child* (Wheaton: SP Publications, 1977), pp. 19-20.
2. Campbell, pp. 20-21.
3. Campbell, pp. 31-32.

61463

4. H. Norman Wright, *Communication: Key to Your Marriage* (Glendale, Calif.: G/L Publications, 1974), pp. 58-59.
5. Mark Lee, "Why Marriages Fail—Communication," in *Make More of Your Marriage,* ed. Gary Collins (Waco, Texas: Word Books, 1976), p. 75.
6. Sven Wahlroos, *Family Communication* (New York: Macmillan Co., 1974), pp. 8-9.

10

Helping Children Communicate Their Feelings

Emotional development begins at birth, or perhaps even prior to birth. Your child's growing self-image will play an important role in the development and demonstration of his emotions. Your child will experience fear, jealousy, anger, sadness, joy, elation, happiness, depression, and many other emotions. Emotions involve the feeling life of a child.

When Johnny opens his birthday present and sees the new toy, he is happy and elated. If Jimmy, his older brother, comes along and takes the toy away from him, Johnny may become angry. Johnny and Jimmy fight over the toy and pull at it and crack! It breaks! Now Johnny is sad and goes to his mother for comfort and sympathy. If this were to happen to you as a parent, how would you respond? What emotions would you share with your child? Would you listen to his emotions and share your own with him? Some parents ignore the feelings and encourage the child to forget his feelings. If this occurs, however, we are not allowing our child to develop as fully as God intended for him to.

Emotions Color Life
Children's emotions develop in different ways. One child de-

velops a balanced emotional life and another child does not. Emotions give color to life. Your child's emotions will have a tremendous influence on his behavior and his attitudes. Emotions may be positive forces which enrich experiences. They can also be a source of motivation and in some instances strength. Mild emotional responses can have a tonic effect upon the mind and increase mental alertness and endurance. A small amount of fear or concern can make a person more alert for study or a performance. On the other hand, emotions can also disorient reality. They can be the cause for creating serious problems of alienation between ourselves and other people.

Emotions can bring parent and child together during the times of happiness, joy, delight, sadness, hurt, or grief. But they can also create distance through the times of anger, rejection, and sadness. There are several responses which affect us as children or adults when we experience *strong* emotions. When our emotions are very intense, for example, they can interfere with our learning.

If a student is overly fearful of failure in school he may find himself studying without grasping the meaning of what he is reading.

A strong emotion tends to inhibit the ability to recall what a person has learned. Take, for example, the individual who studies hard for an exam and really learns the material, but is unable to remember any of the material during the examination because of his intense fear of failure. This individual actually brings about the very thing he is afraid will happen.

Strong emotion narrows perception. When you are very angry you tend to perceive only the elements in the situation that enhance your anger. Your child has been a pest most of the day and you become angry. What you probably see and remember about your child at that moment is only the bad behavior. You overlook the several occasions on this day when your child was helpful and cooperative. The same reaction occurs with fear—you tend to focus on those elements which feed your fear.

During times like these your creative and critical thinking is limited. You are apt to make generalizations and exaggerations. You're angry at your wife and you begin to make accusations. "You're never on time. You're always late and making me be late. No one could be as slow as you." Then you may extend this generalization to her relatives. "You learned to be late because of those slowpokes in your family. I've always noticed that the friends you pick are duds too." And the generalizations continue!

When a person overreacts emotionally he *spends his time thinking about the threat or problem instead of the solution*. A person who has to give an important speech begins to be fearful over making mistakes and creating a bad impression. Now this *is* a possibility. But because of his overconcern with it happening it is ever more likely to occur. It would be much better for him to direct this energy toward learning and practicing the speech. In place of visualizing oneself failing when giving a speech, why not visualize making a successful presentation? Why not go over in one's mind the specific steps necessary to bring about that success?

Strong emotions also tend to reduce the control of behavior by thought. When you have a strong emotion you feel an urge to do something immediately instead of waiting to consider it in the light of accumulated experience. This is the problem of acting first and thinking later. This type of impulsive behavior can bring on greater difficulties.

Several scriptural passages caution against acting first and thinking later. Some of these have to do with speech and our emotions.

"Understand [this] my beloved brethren. Let every man be quick to hear, (a ready listener) slow to speak, slow to take offense and to get angry" (James 1:19, AMP).

"A hot-tempered man stirs up strife, but he who is slow to anger appeases contention" (Prov. 15:18, AMP).

"He who is slow to anger is better than the mighty, and he who rules his own spirit than he who takes a city" (Prov. 16:32, AMP).

Our emotions play a large part in making our lives meaningful or miserable. C. B. Eavey, in his book *Principles of Mental Health for Christian Living,* suggests:

"Nothing in us so defiles and destroys the beauty and the glory of living as do emotions; nothing so elevates, purifies, enriches, and strengthens life as does emotion. Through our emotions we can have the worst or the best, we can descend to the lowest depths, or we can rise to the highest heights. Every normal human being has a longing for the overflowing of natural emotion. Without capacity to experience emotions suitable to the situations we meet, we would not be normal. Emotions of the right kind, expressed in the proper way, make life beautiful, full, and rich, rob it of monotony, and contribute much to both the enjoyment and the effectiveness of living." [1]

Our emotions are a gift from God for we were created as emotional beings. Because of the fall, man's emotional life often becomes distorted. But our emotions as such should never be despised, expelled, ignored, or even neglected. "If we try to drive out any one of them," adds Eavey, "we simply intensify its activity. When we let them go without guidance and control, they cause confusion and riot in our lives. If we try to suppress them, they produce destruction in our personalities."

For better or for worse, our emotions are an important part of us. Whether they are *better* or *worse* depends upon our use of them. [2]

Used Emotions

Did you know that emotional responses serve a purpose for a child? Did you know that there are actual goals which can be achieved through emotional responses? Our emotions give us more power and intensity. A child learns this quite early. He learns that his emotions can get what he wants or help him to overpower another person. If your child's crying breaks down your resistance toward a new doll in a store, she may use crying again. Your child may learn that if he looks sad and begins to cry when you ask him to turn off the TV and go to bed, that you may give in for another 15 minutes of TV watching. The authors of the excellent book *Raising a Responsible Child* have suggested the following goals of emotions:

a. To get special attention
b. To control a situation
c. To retaliate for supposed unfair treatment
d. To protect oneself from having to perform.[3]

Unused Emotions

Some families in our society still live with the problem of alienated emotions. If parents were raised in families that were head-oriented, producing an atmosphere that downgraded feelings, the emotions were then relegated toward the sex roles. Women had feelings and emotions, and men were strong. Men were taught to be tough (which meant not to show much emotion, especially of the tender variety). However, displays of anger *were* acceptable for men.

We seem to have a tendency even to mistrust some who demonstrate too great a show of emotions. We associate open expressions of emotions with poor judgment. Unfortunately this is associated especially with women. Reactions have been voiced against having a woman president or a woman airline pilot; there is a fear of how they would respond emotionally under stress.

A husband or father who is alienated from his own feelings cannot accept emotional expressions from others. This creates two problems for his family. He denies good emotional acceptance and expression in his own family and he has difficulty in satisfying the needs of his child and spouse for affection. Gentle emotions such as kindness, affection, appreciation, compassion, reverence, concern, wistfulness, and sadness may not only not be demonstrated by the father but unappreciated when shared by others in his household. The alienation of emotions is something that we have learned. Getting in touch with our emotions can be learned too.

Are You in Touch?

Let's check to see what you believe and feel about emotions. Write your answers to the following questions.

1. Do I feel it's all right to express my feelings and emotions and to talk about them? Do I feel that feelings and emotions are bad? How would my spouse answer these questions? What do my children believe and feel? What have I done specifically to teach them about emotions and feelings?

2. Do I allow my emotions to emerge within me naturally and without trying to push them down? Do I feel that I have to make up emotions that I don't feel to please others or because I think I should feel this way? How would my spouse answer these questions? How do my children feel and how would they answer these questions?

3. Are there any emotions that I overdo, and if so what are they? Are there emotions that I refuse to show or allow to be demonstrated in my presence? Which emotions do my spouse and children show and which bother me?

4. Do I let my emotions enter into my speech and communication or is there too much control? Do I know how to put feelings into words? Does my spouse? Do my children?

5. Do I use my emotions to get what I want or to cause others to leave me alone? Does my spouse? Do my children? Which emotions are used?

6. Do I talk about my emotions when they arise or do I wait until another time when I might feel safer? Does my spouse? Do my children? Which emotions do I express immediately and which do I delay?

7. True or false. I believe I have the right to express any of my emotions at any time as long as I don't step on the rights of others. Do I ever violate the rights of others by the use of my emotions? Do I feel that my spouse or my children do?

8. Am I willing to take risks in expressing my emotions? Do I still express them if others become upset or blame me for the problem that is being created? Can I express emotions without losing control? Can my spouse? Can my children? Describe a time when you expressed your anger in a healthy way.

9. How do I feel when others are expressing their emotions? Have I ever or do I usually try to get others *not* to express their emotions? Am I a feeling-stopper?

10. Which emotions are the most difficult for me to express? How can my family members help me in expressing these? Which emotions are the most difficult for my spouse or children to express?

Expressing Your Feelings

Many people have difficulty expressing certain types of feelings. Here are some of those feelings. Let's see how you would deal with these issues. Take each topic listed here and write what you would say to express this feeling. If your child feels like this, what does he or she do to express this feeling? Could he or she be expressing it already and you not be catching it? Think about it.

Feelings about not being able to do things
Feelings about not being able to change a situation
Feelings of jealousy
Feelings of not being able to handle compliments or affection
Feelings of being hurt or rejected
Feelings of wanting to punish someone
Feelings of guilt or a need to be punished
Feelings of shame

Feelings of helplessness
Feelings of disappointment
Feelings of depression
Feelings of being a worthwhile person and valued by others
Feelings of being inadequate

11. How do I feel about myself? Are my feelings positive or negative? How do I feel about other family members? These feelings toward myself or others, and how they are expressed, will affect my emotional life.[4]

Let's explore this last point in a bit more detail. You may begin to identify some of these next suggestions as being present either in your own life or in the life of one of your children.

Self-image Results

If a parent or a child feels that he is "no-good," he may hesitate to develop friendships with others. Part of the thinking that occurs in the person's mind is that a friendship means giving yourself to the other person, and nobody wants a gift that isn't good.

• If a parent or child feels bad about himself, he may try to keep others at a distance because of not feeling worthy.

• If a parent or child feels bad about himself, he may feel quite lonely and desire closeness with people. But he behaves in such a manner that he drives others away because of coming on too strong.

• If a parent or child feels good about himself, he will make friends quite readily and allow others to be his friends.

• If a parent or child feels that he is a weak person who has many needs, he will present this image to others. He will also let others know, in one way or another, that he has many needs but very little resource to give to others.

• If a parent or child has a lot of problems that he cannot handle, he will expect others to listen to his problems but will probably be a poor listener himself. He will expect others to be helpers more than friends.

• If a parent or child feels he is better than other people, he will have difficulty in being an open, honest, and disclosing communicator. He will make few attempts to understand others, especially if he feels they do not meet his standards.

How Do You Feel?

It is important that young children learn about emotions and how to adequately express them. Listed here are a number of emotions. Complete this assignment first by yourself and then with your own children. Take each of these feelings and make three statements about the feeling. Try to use adjectives to describe what you really feel and what is going on inside you. For example, you are angry. How could you describe this? You could say, "I feel upset. I am bothered and irritated. I feel tense and jumpy. I feel like yelling or crying because I am frustrated. I feel like I am being taken advantage of by these kids and I want to tell them what I think." Now you may notice that in this description we used short and long phrases and we also described what was happening to cause the anger and what the person wanted to do. These are important steps in helping our children learn to communicate their feelings.

After you (and your spouse) have worked through this list, plan a time to talk with your child about these feelings. Ask him to describe them, or make a game of it by sharing your responses together. Or take some blank pieces of paper and crayons and each of you draw (literally or symbolically) how you feel when you experience this emotion. Share your picture with one another and then verbally describe the feelings. This is a helpful way to allow people to think about their feelings and helps them put their feelings into words.

Embarrassed	Guilty	Depressed
Loving	Affectionate	Afraid
Worried	Fearful	Frustrated
Helpful	Hurt	Joyful

Jealous	Inferior	Lonely
Accepted	Rejected	Defensive
Disappointed	Sad	Shy
Trustworthy	Mistrusted	Angry

Another way of helping a child express his feelings is to use a sentence-completion form and make a game of finishing the sentences. Here are some examples. You can probably think of others that would be interesting for your own family situation. Each person should share the first response that comes to mind without thinking a long time about what he will say.

I like myself best when . . .
I feel upset about myself when . . .
I get angry at ——————— when . . .
I get angry with myself when . . .
When I do something right I feel . . .
When I fail I feel . . .
I feel good when . . .
I feel bad when . . .
I feel happy when . . .
I feel sad when . . .
I am scared when . . .
I feel safe when . . .

References

1. C. B. Eavey, *Principles of Mental Health for Christian Living* (Chicago: Moody Press, 1957).
2. H. Norman Wright, *The Christian Use of Emotional Power* (Old Tappan, N.J.: Fleming H. Revell, 1974), pp. 20-22.
3. Don Dinkmeyer and Gary McKay, *Raising a Responsible Child* (New York: Simon & Schuster, 1973), pp. 36-37.
4. Adapted from Gerard Egan, *You and Me* (Monterey, Calif.: Brooks Cole, 1977), p. 85.

11

Helping Children Accept and Release
Their Fear and Anger

How can you deal with specific emotions or feelings? Two of
the most common emotions are fear and anger, and they
warrant some discussion. It is normal for a young child to
experience fear at some time. Unexpected noises, the sudden
arrival of a stranger, or entering unfamiliar places may bring
on this feeling. That is normal. Fear is also necessary for a
child to learn to survive. However, because of a child's lack
of ability at certain ages to perceive and because of his
creative imagination, some of the fears may not be valid. As
parents you can help him distinguish what is and what is not
a valid fear. If you are a fearful person, your child may
acquire fears from your example and feelings. In fact, you
may teach your child to be overly afraid.

Understanding Your Child's Fear
When your child expresses fear he needs someone who will
listen and understand. *Understanding* here means seeing
through the eyes of the child. If a child can share what his
fears are and talk them out with a person who will *not*
ridicule him or tell him not to have the feelings, if he can tell
them to a person who can empathize with him and reflect

113

what he is feeling and help him verbalize his fears, he will feel better and be more open to doing something about them. He will be more open to suggestions and support from his parents. Never laugh at a child's fear nor use it to manipulate him.

You want to be able to convey to your child through your listening that you can understand. Then you want to move to the next step with your child, which is, "What do you think that we can do about what you are afraid of?" Working with a child to develop a plan (depending on the maturity of the child) to face and overcome the subject of the fear will take time and patience, but this will teach your child skills which can be used in other situations.

Here is an example of what one parent worked out to say to her six-year-old child when she wanted to talk with him about fear. You may want to think about sharing something similar with your own child if there is a need. You may stop and have the child respond to some of these questions as you go along.

Boys and girls are sometimes afraid. They are afraid of different things. Some are afraid of the dark. Are you? Some are afraid of dogs. Are you? Some are afraid of loud noises. Are you? They are also afraid of things that could happen to them. They might be afraid of other boys and girls. Perhaps they won't play with them or like them.

What is it like to be afraid? What does fear feel like? Most people don't like fear because it makes things happen in their body. Your stomach might feel funny. Your legs might shake and your heart beats faster and louder. Has that ever happened to you? Your fear is telling the body to get ready for action. What does a person's face look like when he is afraid? Can you tell when a person is frightened?

Is fear good for anything? Sometimes. Some of your fears keep you from harm. Most people are afraid of running into the street or freeway without looking. Most children are afraid of picking up a rattlesnake. We have taught you to be afraid of some things which might hurt you. Can you think of a fear that you like? Maybe you have seen a scary monster show on TV or at the movies. Children like to scream at this. But most of them know that there is nothing to really be afraid of either.

Do you know what you can do when you are afraid? Most children either run away from what they are afraid of or they fight it. If another child is a bully you may run from him or you may fight him. You may want to stay home or even pretend you are sick to get out of something that you are afraid of. Perhaps you could talk about your fear to us or to a friend. Perhaps you could really find out if you need to be afraid of it. Perhaps that person isn't so much of a bully after all. Perhaps that dog that we are afraid of isn't so mean after all and if we walk up to him with his owner he would be friendly.

What are you afraid of? What do you do? What would you like to do with your fears? [1]

If you find that you as a parent or one of your children is a worrier, let me suggest a book I have written which speaks to this topic: *An Answer to Worry and Anxiety* (Harvest House, 1976).

Anger

The second emotion to be considered is anger. Many people do not understand anger. They feel that it is always wrong and should either not be found in a child or should be gotten rid of as soon as we see any sign of it. Do you know what anger is? Do you know what causes it, either in you or your child?

A simple definition of *anger* is a strong feeling of irritation or displeasure, which is usually temporary. Your reaction to anger may be displayed openly or retained inside. You can be just as angry while keeping silent as you can while yelling at someone, and so can your child.

The words *rage* and *fury* are used to describe intense, uncontained, explosive emotion. Fury is thought of as being destructive, but rage can be considered justified by certain circumstances. Have you seen either of these in your child?

Another word for anger is *wrath*—fervid anger that seeks vengeance or punishment. *Resentment* is usually used to signify suppressed anger brought about by a sense of grievance. *Indignation* is a feeling which results when you see the mistreatment of someone or something which is very important to you.

Anger in the Bible

The Word of God has much to say about anger and uses a number of words to describe the various types of anger. In the Old Testament, the word for anger actually meant "nostril" or "nose." In ancient Hebrew psychology the nose was thought to be the seat of anger. The phrase *slow to anger* literally means "long of nose." Synonyms used in the Old Testament for anger include ill-humor and rage (Esther 1:12), overflowing rage and fury (Amos 1:11), and indignation (Jer. 15:17). The emotion of anger can be the subject of the Scripture even though the exact word is not present. Anger can be implied through words such as revenge, cursing, jealousy, snorting, trembling, shouting, raving, and grinding the teeth.

Several words are used for anger in the New Testament. It is important to note the distinctions between these words. Many people have concluded that the Scripture contradicts itself because in one verse we are taught not to be angry and in another we are admonished to "be angry and sin not." Which is correct and which should we follow? (Note: When your child is old enough to understand, he should learn the scriptural guidelines for anger.)

One of the words used most often for anger in the New Testament is *thumas,* "a turbulent commotion or a boiling agitation of feelings." This type of anger blazes up into a sudden explosion. It is an outburst from inner indignation and is similar to a match which quickly ignites into a blaze but then burns out rapidly. This type of anger is mentioned 20 times in passages such as Ephesians 4:31 and Galatians 5:20. We are to control this type of anger. How could you help your child with this type of anger?

Another type of anger mentioned only three times in the New Testament, and never in a positive sense, is *parorgismos*. This is anger that has been provoked and is characterized by irritation, exasperation, or embitterment.

"Do not ever let your wrath—your exasperation, your fury or indignation—last until the sun goes down" (Eph. 4:26b, AMP).

"Again I ask, Did Israel not understand?—Did the Jews have no warning that the Gospel was to go forth to the Gentiles, to all the earth? First, there is Moses who says, 'I will make you jealous of those who are not a nation; with a foolish nation I will make you angry' " (Rom. 10:19, AMP).

The most common New Testament word for anger is *orge*. It is used 45 times and means "a more settled and long-lasting attitude which is slower in its onset but more enduring, often including revenge." This kind of anger is similar to coals on a barbecue slowly warming up to red and then white hot and holding this temperature until the cooking is done.

There are only two times that this word is used where revenge is not included in its meaning. In Ephesians 4:26b we are taught not to "let the sun go down on your anger" (NASB). Mark 3:5 records Jesus as having looked on the Pharisees "with anger" (NASB). In these two verses the word means "an abiding and sealed habit of the mind which is aroused under certain conditions against evil and injustice." This is the type of anger that Christians are encouraged to have—the anger that includes no revenge.

The basic overall theme of Scripture concerning anger is that it will be a part of life. It is not to be denied, but it is to be controlled. Certain types of anger are not healthy and should be put away. Anger should be aroused against definite injustices and then used properly.

What about the type of anger that you and your child experience? What is it like? How would you classify it as you read over these definitions again? [2]

Causes of Anger

What are the causes of anger? They fall into three basic categories. *Fear* can bring on anger. Anger is a reaction against what you are afraid of. For some reason people seem to be more comfortable with anger than fear. The anger is almost like a symptom of a code telling you that something else is bothering you. When your child is angry do you always respond to the anger or do you attempt to discover what is behind it? Your child's anger may be telling you something else.

Another basic reason for anger is *hurt*. When you experience emotional or physical hurt, the response quickly turns to anger. Look at the following diagram. As illustrated by the diagram, the intensity and awareness of hurt feelings accelerate rapidly seconds after the event that caused them. The anger quickly begins to grow more intense. This feeling peaks out above the emotion of hurt in just a few seconds and then the third response occurs—the desire to hurt or revenge. If this lingers it turns to bitterness or resentment, which may hurt the one with the feelings more than the person it is against.

The third major cause of anger is *frustration*. Frustration occurs in many forms. It is a condition of wanting something and not getting it. Your child may experience frustration in the areas of his wishes, desires, ambitions, hopes, hungers, instinct, and even his will. He may often respond with anger. If he is hungry and cannot eat, he may become angry. If he is frightened by something and cannot run away, he may become angry.

When your child is frustrated he needs to discover the

Hurt and Anger: Knowing the Difference[3]

The interaction of hurt, anger, and revengefulness

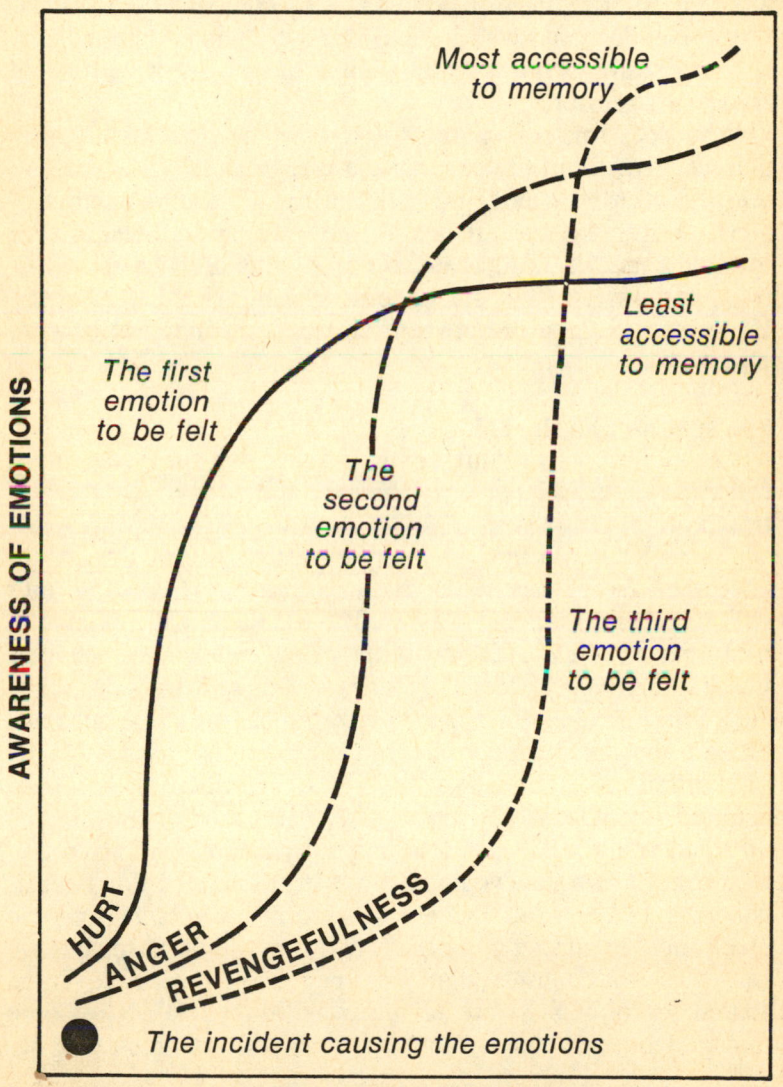

Most accessible to memory

Least accessible to memory

The first emotion to be felt

The second emotion to be felt

The third emotion to be felt

AWARENESS OF EMOTIONS

HURT

ANGER

REVENGEFULNESS

The incident causing the emotions

THE PASSING OF TIME

source of his frustration. Objects, situations, or other people may be the cause. His friends, father, mother, brother or sister could be the source of frustration. One can be frustrated just as easily by someone he loves as by someone he dislikes.

Your child could also be frustrated by what some call the laws of nature. If he is hungry he could be frustrated by an empty refrigerator.

Why does frustration lead to anger? The basic assumption that we have about life can cause anger to arise out of frustration. Frustration may begin with desire—"I want something." Now, desires are natural; we all have wants and desires. We set goals and we want them to come true. But we must distinguish between "I want something" and "I must have it." If you can distinguish between the two, you may not become so upset.

Frustration and the Bible

The Scriptures provide some insight into the problem of frustration. Several passages indicate the proper response to frustration:

"Consider it wholly joyful, my brethren, whenever you are enveloped in or encounter trials of any sort, or fall into various temptations. Be assured and understand that the trial and proving of your faith bring out endurance and steadfastness and patience" (James 1:2-3, AMP).

"(You should) be exceedingly glad on this account, though now for a little while you may be distressed by trials and suffer temptations, so that (the genuineness) of your faith may be tested" (1 Peter 1:6-7, AMP).

When you say "I want something," you are sometimes saying, "I must have it. I've got to have it or else. If I don't get it, it's going to be awful. I've got to have my way, and if people block me they are terrible. In fact, if they don't let me get my way, then that's just a sign that they don't love me." These statements only help create anger within you. You assume that you have to have your way, and you are frustrated because hindrances to satisfaction are in your way—and shouldn't be.

Perhaps we should ask the question, "Why not?" Why shouldn't you experience frustration just like anyone else? You are not immune to it. It can be a growth experience. And it will be if you add another phrase to the initial statement, "I want something." "I want something, but it is all right if I don't get it. It is not the end of the world. I can live without it and can adjust and find an alternative."

Learning to live without something can often bring a greater level of satisfaction to life. This is not to say that you totally give up and never forge ahead. It is just that you do not allow yourself to become upset by the various frustrations of life. If you do, the result is an emotional response which most people call anger.[4]

As your child develops in age and maturity, the understanding and application of the Scriptures mentioned before may help him deal with his life situations in a healthy manner. When your child is angry, instead of reacting to his anger, listen to him. Help him talk it out. Begin to discover if he is afraid of something. Find out if he has experienced hurt. Discover his frustration. Help him learn constructive ways of dealing with his anger. There are several ways to handle it.

Dealing with Anger

One way is to *repress* it. Don't even admit that you are angry. Ignore its presence. This repression is often unconscious, but it is *not healthy!* Repressing anger is like placing a wastebasket full of paper in a closet and setting fire to it. The fire will either burn itself out *or* it could set the entire house on fire and burn it down. The energy produced by anger cannot be destroyed. It must be converted or directed into another channel.

One outlet for repressed anger is accidents. Perhaps you have met people who are *accident-prone*. Unfortunately, their accidents may involve other people as well as themselves. A child who is angry may slam a door on his own hand or someone else's. A child may wash windows for his parent when he would rather be watching a game on TV and put his hand through the window.

Anger and hatred can lead to further complications, but so does repression. Repressed anger or anger turned inward often turns into depression. In an unconscious attempt to handle the emotion, you bring harm to your own body; your children may learn to repress anger too.

A second way to handle anger is to *suppress* it. A person choosing this means is aware of his anger but chooses to hold it in and not let people know he is angry. In some situations this may be healthy and wise, but eventually the anger needs to be recognized and drained away in a healthy manner. Otherwise the storage apparatus will begin to overflow at the wrong time and place.

Children learn indirect ways to let their anger out when they have not been given healthy outlets. Constant teasing, sarcasm or tattling may be used. They may find some substitute targets too—cruelty to animals, reactions to younger children or younger siblings, learning to take it out on themselves through physical acts of violence, or becoming depressed.

Often a person chooses to suppress his anger when the person with whom he is angry could react with strong force or authority.

Suppressing anger does have some merit, especially if it helps you relax, cool down, and begin to act in a rational manner. The Word of God has something to say about this type of suppression.

"He who is slow to anger has great understanding, but he who is hasty of spirit exposes and exalts his folly" (Prov. 14:29, AMP).

"A hot-tempered man stirs up strife, but he who is slow to anger appeases contention" (Prov. 15:18, AMP).

"He who is slow to anger is better than the mighty, and he

who rules his own spirit than he who takes a city" (Prov. 16:32, AMP).

"Good sense makes a man restrain his anger, and it is his glory to overlook a transgression or an offense" (Prov. 19:11, AMP).

"Make no friendships with a man given to anger, and with a wrathful man do not associate" (Prov. 22:24, AMP).

"I (Nehemiah) was very angry when I heard their cry and these words. I thought it over, then rebuked the nobles and officials" (Neh. 5:6-7a, AMP).

"Understand (this), my beloved brethren. Let every man be quick to hear, (a ready listener) slow to speak, slow to take offense and to get angry" (James 1:19, AMP).

A child who practices and exerts self-control will find that his anger level actually decreases. He will not become *as* angry as if he were to simply cut loose with his first reaction. A calm consideration of the cause for the anger and the results will help him handle a situation properly.

Expressing anger is a third way to handle it. Some people think you should express exactly what you feel, no matter who or what is involved. They feel this is psychologically healthy and absolutely necessary in order to live a balanced life.

There are many different ways to express anger. One is to react with violent passion, yelling harsh words, swearing, all with tremendous emotion. This can bring results but you may not care for them. If you are allowed the freedom to react in this way, shouldn't the other person have the same freedom to react to you in this manner? A young child may scream, hit, shove, bite, spit, or pinch. A temper tantrum may be used by the child to express his anger.

But you can also express your anger by riding your bike around the block, digging in the garden for an hour, or beating on a stuffed pillow. You can write down exactly how you feel when you get angry, especially if it is difficult to verbalize your feelings. These methods may sound strange but they should not be discounted. They have been used to help many people overcome their difficulties with anger.[5]

If your child can learn to accept his anger and talk it out or confess it to someone who understands or the person involved, he will have discovered the healthiest way of all. If he can learn to look at the causes for his anger, this too will assist him in learning in the future to control his reactions and respond in a constructive manner.

Expressions of Feelings

As a parent you will often hear expressions of feelings from your children that are unacceptable to you. These feelings may anger or alarm you and your immediate response may be to want to eliminate either the feeling or its expression from your child. There are several schools of thought concerning the expression of feelings. Some would suggest letting a child express whatever he is feeling at that time, using his own choice of words. The parent would encourage the child to get out his feelings and assist him by reflecting what he has said and helping him work out the expression.

Some suggest that parents not help the child work out what he is going to do with his feelings. In a conflict between your child and another, you would not help them resolve the differences. Others suggest that such feelings and such expressions of feelings have no place in the Christian life and therefore should be hit head-on, and the child disciplined immediately for even having such thoughts, let alone expressing them.

How do you handle the expression of feelings? What have you done in the past and what has been the result? Let's consider an example that might give us some guidelines. Johnny is seven years old and has just hit his younger brother, Jimmy, who is five. Jimmy cries and goes running to his mother to tell her about it. Mother comes in looking upset and asks Johnny why he hit his brother. Johnny says, "He broke one of my toys again. He always does that. I hate him. I hate him. I wish he didn't live here!" How would you respond in this situation? What would you say? Before reading on, think about how you would respond.

Many parents would respond with something like: "How can you say such bad things about your brother? You know it is wrong to hate! What have we told you about that? Haven't you learned anything in Sunday School? Your brother is a nice boy and he cares for you. He didn't mean to break your toy. He is just younger than you and hasn't learned how to handle them as well as you have. You should know better than to hit him. Young man, go to your room! There is no television for you for three days! You stay in your room until you are sorry and apologize to your brother!"

Have you heard this before? Many of us have said something similar or have had it said to us when we were younger. There are some parents who ask, "Well, isn't that the way to handle it? You can't let a child go around telling his brothers and sisters that he hates them and then hitting them!" Let's look at what Mother said and analyze some problems in this approach.

1. What is Mother scolding Johnny for? For his feelings just as much as for what he has done. What is this saying to her son? Basically, that he should not tell her about how he feels in the future as he is going to get jumped on for feeling that way. Many children have learned not to express their anger, hurt, or resentful feelings to their parents because of getting lashed at. This then denies parents the opportunity to assist a child in working through these normal feelings which we all have experienced at one time or another.

2. Mother is apparently not making an attempt to understand his feelings at this time. In fact, she is saying that she cannot understand why he would feel that way because his brother is such a nice child. She is implying that Johnny's feelings are hard to understand. Since understanding feelings is an important step in controlling feelings, what is this saying to her son?

3. Mother is also taking sides because of the age of the children. She is assuming that Jimmy is weaker and incapable of knowing what he was doing. He is therefore the underdog. But is this always true? Some younger children purposely set up a reaction from an older brother or sister simply to get the other person into trouble. Mother is telling her older son that his brother didn't really know what he was doing, but Johnny may know better. A younger child is not always less adept at getting older children into trouble. Jimmy may know that he can get his brother into difficulty. If you find patterns like this occurring with your children, consider the possibility.

4. How does Johnny feel about his mother's reaction? He could feel resentment, unfairness, guilt or humiliation. How does he feel about having to feel sorry and apologize? How does he feel about Jimmy who is apparently getting off scot-free at this time?

5. Mother has not really done anything to prevent this same problem from occurring in the future. Perhaps Jimmy needs some guidelines or controls about playing with the toys. Johnny may not feel that his toys are protected and he may resent his brother playing with them because he knows it's going to happen again.

Alternative Responses

What could have been said? Here are two possible responses by Mother. Mother comes in and asks Johnny why he hit his brother. Johnny said, "He broke one of my toys again. He always does that. I hate him. I hate him. I wish he didn't live here." Mother: "I can understand that you are mad at Jimmy for breaking your toy. I will do whatever I can to see that he doesn't break any of your toys again. If necessary I will tell him that he will be disciplined the next time it happens. I would rather that you come and tell me and let me handle it than you hitting him. I would like you to promise me that you will not hit Jimmy again, and I will promise you that I will do as much as I can to help Jimmy realize that he must take care of your toys. Now what do you feel about my suggestions? What do you feel should be done about the problem at this time?"

Another approach might be, "Johnny, I believe that you know the rule that neither of you can hit the other. I know that you are upset over Jimmy breaking your toy, but I want you to let me handle a problem like this. Because you hit him, you will be (whatever discipline you use) and Jimmy will receive the same because he has been told not to play with your toys unless he has your permission. I can understand how you are upset. Would you like to talk now about what we can do in the future to prevent this from occurring again, or would you like to talk about it later?"

These approaches are different, yet there are constructive elements in both. You may have some other positive suggestions, or you may disagree. Your concept of discipline may be different. The communication process involved in these two suggestions and the previous one is really what I am asking you to observe. The communication of feelings and the reaction or response to them is very critical.

Let's analyze what was shared in these last two examples.

1. Johnny's feelings were respected and he was not attacked for having them. You may want to suggest that he learn to express his feelings in more acceptable words. At another time when he is not feeling angry with his brother, you might engage him in a conversation about how he feels about Jimmy. You might reflect on times when he has said that he hates him and talk over whether these are occasional responses because of the problem or whether that is what he is really feeling or meaning at that time. He may surprise you and say that he really doesn't mean that, but he was so upset at that moment he didn't know what to say. That would be your opportunity to suggest mature words. You may suggest some alternatives to replace *hate*, etc.

2. These examples also indicate Jimmy's responsibility in the matter and they do not try to convince Johnny that his

brother is nice. Johnny knows that he isn't nice, from his point of view, since his toys are broken.

3. Here Mother is trying to help both of them with the problem. She is trying to assist, so that hopefully the number of times that this occurs will be cut down.[6]

References

1. Carl Fischer, *What About Me?* (Cincinnati: Pfalum-Standard, 1972), pp. 33-37.
2. Adapted from Norman Wright, *An Answer to Anger and Frustration* (Irvine, Calif.: Harvest House, 1977), pp. 11-14.
3. Paul Welter, *Family Problems and Predicaments: How to Respond* (Wheaton: Tyndale House, 1977), p. 130.
4. Wright, *Anger,* pp. 308.
5. Wright, *Anger,* pp. 30-41.
6. Adapted from Sven Wahlroos, *Family Communication* (New York: Macmillan Co., 1974), pp. 154-157.

12

Principles of Communication

The pattern of communication that develops in a family depends on many factors. Your marriage is the foundation of communication for the whole family. The atmosphere you establish will determine whether communication is constructive or destructive in your family. Your communication habits as a parent are the model your children will learn from as they develop their own ways of communicating. Though the words themselves don't always explain them, emotions are one of the major elements communicated between family members. As you develop your skill and discipline in expressing yourself, communication will increasingly work for your family instead of being a source of problems

Avoid Nagging
One of the major communication problems in families is nagging. Often a husband comes in for counseling and says that his wife nags him. I ask what he means by nag. He replies, "Every week she asks me to clean the garage." Now this really doesn't sound much like nagging. It sounds more like reminding, especially if it is a well-expressed request. We need to note the difference between nagging and reminding.

Nagging has been defined as "a continual, persistent, critical faultfinding which creates irritation in another person." One person defined nagging as reminding a person to do something when you know he hasn't forgotten. It has also been expressed as inefficiency on our part to promote the desired behavior in another. Nagging is a negative verbal behavior that has very little communication value.

What is the difference between nagging and frequent reminders? Nagging usually continues on and on and on, but frequent reminders lead to learning. Most children when they are young need reminding because they do not have a ready-made, built-in sense of responsibility. (For that matter, many adults lack this as well!) A sense of responsibility is learned through day-by-day activities, but it is not always easy to learn. The impulses of a child are quite strong, and he needs to rely on outside controls. Couple that with a short attention span, and the tendency to become so preoccupied with what he is interested in, and it is no wonder that he needs reminding.

Husbands and wives experience nagging in terms of being continually reminded to do something. Usually the tone of voice indicates the difference between reminding and nagging. Husbands are nagged about taking out the garbage, cleaning the garage, cutting the grass, cleaning the yard, picking up the socks, etc. Wives are nagged about having dinner on time, overcooking the steak, picking up the soap and shampoo in the shower, taking clothes to the cleaners, etc. What do you think children are nagged about? Think of five or six frequent nagging behaviors.

Does nagging accomplish anything? Some say no, but this isn't true. Nagging does bring results, but they are usually negative. Nagging encourages a spouse to continue to engage in the very behavior he or she is being nagged about. This behavior leads to quarrels and resentment. It also leads the other person to develop a strange malady—a form of deafness known as tuning out the spouse. Nagging is as common as the flu and, like a communicable disease, it makes all of the family members miserable.

Reasons for Nagging

What causes parents to fall into the trap of nagging? Here are several suggestions which have been given by Dr. Sven Wahlroos:

1. Parents may have unrealistic expectations concerning the abilities of a child or the amount of work that he is expected to accomplish. If this is true, then many children will not respond, since they feel they are overwhelmed or will fail the task anyway.

2. Children and parents often like to show their power, and not doing something that one is asked to do is a good way to demonstrate this.

3. A third cause concerns how parents state rules or make requests. You need to be very clear and definitive in your statements and also expect the same from your child. When he says he will do it later, always clarify what he means by the word *later*.

4. Procrastination may develop on the part of a child because he was not informed of the consequences of not doing what he was told.[1]

The Scriptures warn against nagging. "Love forgets mistakes; nagging about them parts the best of friends" (Prov. 17:9, LB). "It is better to dwell in a corner of the housetop (on the flat oriental roof, exposed to all kinds of weather) than in a house shared with a nagging, quarrelsome and faultfinding woman" (Prov. 21:9, AMP).

Minimizing Nagging

Here are some steps toward minimizing nagging (if you happen to use this method), and ways to respond to one who nags you.

1. Distinguish between nagging and reminding. A reminder remains friendly, with no tone of irritation, impa-

tience, or anger. Nagging usually involves destructive means of communication such as the use of exaggeration, sarcasm, humiliation, and playing the numbers game. "You will never do what I ask you to do!" "A moron could remember to follow instructions better than you do." "If I've told you once, I have told you a thousand times."

Although people attempt to use nagging as a means of communicating and motivating, it doesn't work. Instead of recognizing this fact and employing a different means, they intensify their efforts and nag all the more!

Nagging can become a habit. When you fail to get another person's attention before speaking to him, he will probably appear to ignore you. When you yell from one room to another without making sure the person is listening, can you blame him for lack of response? Sometimes he may hear you and sometimes not. If you allow this pattern to continue, he will soon learn that when you ask him to do something, all he needs to do is tune you out, perhaps even pretend not to hear. With practice he may learn not to hear. The end result is that he learns how to control you by not listening.

2. Another reason for nagging is that we accept ambiguous answers or responses. If a child answers a request by saying, "I will do it later," tell him you don't know what he means by later; to avoid any misunderstanding, you would like to know the exact time. If remembering has been a problem for him, suggest writing a reminder note to help him remember. Always insist on clear communication and definite responses.

Dr. Sven Wahlroos tells the story of a couple who came to see him for counseling. The wife constantly nagged her husband about things that needed to be fixed around the house. He would just postpone them and would not allow the wife to call anyone to repair these items because he wanted to save the money. An agreement was worked out with the couple. When the wife noticed that something needed to be fixed, she would bring it to her husband's attention and they would discuss it. The husband then had 15 days in which to fix it. The couple initialed the calendar date so they would remember when they talked about it. During the 15 days, the wife was not to mention it again, as the responsibility was the husband's. At the end of 15 days, if the item was not repaired, the wife could call in a repairman to fix it. You may want to adapt this idea to use with your children.

3. One way that a family can change some of the nagging behavior that occurs is to define and clarify responsibilities for each person. Perhaps questions could be asked such as, "What are the jobs or tasks which need to be done and when should they be done and by whom?" For many couples, discussing responsibilities has helped to solve problems in areas which have been irritants for many years.

Some couples have created a chart describing the division of labor, with jobs and times when they could be done. The purpose of such a chart is to clarify individual responsibilities. Either spouse should comment on the other's failure to do his or her job.

4. Establish automatic rules which cover the subjects over which there has been nagging. When the consequences for either complying with the request or not responding to it have been spelled out, the procrastinating child will feel a greater motivation to respond. The nagging should be eliminated because if the child follows the rules there is no need for nagging or reminding, and if the child does not respond there is no need for nagging as the consequences for that behavior have been spelled out for him as well.

5. Decide if the nagging or reminding is about important or unimportant matters. Decide in your own mind which are important and concentrate upon those. For a while, at least, ignore the others. You might want to discuss the list of rules or behaviors with your child if he or she is old enough to respond.

6. Be sure that you have your child's attention. Don't do anything while you are talking that might distract his attention.

You may want to place your hand gently on the child's shoulder, look into his eyes, speak in a slow distinct voice, and then ask the child to tell you what you said![2]

Being Honest

Honesty or truthfulness rates high on the list of personal qualities that parents want to see expressed in their own children. This characteristic is more likely to come about when two factors are present: a model of honesty and truthfulness on the part of parents, and a child who is secure in himself and in his place within the family. The Word of God has much to say concerning honesty, falsehood, and being truthful. Look at just a few of the many passages found in the Scriptures.

"He who speaks truth tells what is right, but a false witness, deceit" (Prov. 12:17, NASB).

"Lying lips are an abomination to the Lord, but those who deal faithfully are His delight" (Prov. 12:22, NASB).

"Righteous lips are the delight of kings, and he who speaks right is loved" (Prov. 16:13, NASB).

"A false witness will not go unpunished, and he who tells lies will not escape" (Prov. 19:5, NASB).

"Like a madman who throws firebrands, arrows, and death, so is the man who deceives his neighbor, and says, 'Was I not joking?' " (Prov. 26:18-19, NASB)

"In the end, people appreciate frankness more than flattery" (Prov. 28:33, LB).

"Do not lie to one another, since you laid aside the old self with its evil practices" (Col. 3:9, NASB). Any kind of dishonesty, lying or deception is to be dropped from the Christian pattern of living, for all of these behaviors are associated with a non-Christian pattern of behavior.

Ephesians 4:25 and 4:15 are two other strong passages of Scripture on this subject. "Therefore, laying aside falsehood, speak truth, each one of you, with his neighbor, for we are members of one another" (NASB). "But speaking the truth in love. . . ." (NASB) This passage carries with it the dimension of tactfulness or sensitivity. One commentator suggested that a thought presented here is that when the truth is spoken, it should cement together a relationship better than it was before.

The truth should not damage or hurt others. Often under the guise of truth we hurt others. Some humiliate others and then give the excuse that what they said was true. It may be true, but should it have been said in that way? A mother notices that her son's room is messy and she goes outside where he is playing with his friends and says, "Billy! Come in here right now! Your room is a mess and you know that you cannot play until you do your job!" If a child hears this again and again, it can begin to have an effect upon him in a negative way, especially if his friends hear it. Notice the difference in this approach, which can accomplish the same goal but actually help the child by providing a model of good communication: "Billy, you forgot to clean your room. Our rule is that you need to do it before you can play. Please come in and do it now and then you can go back to playing. Thank you." Statements such as "You're too young," "You won't be able to do that," "You can't do that as well as I can," and "You look terrible the way you are dressed" may all be true, but do they need to be said in that way?

Subtle Lies

One of the most subtle ways of lying can be found in the questions we ask of one another. You may wonder, "How can a question be a form of lying?" Often a question is not really an honest question. We have a devious motive behind the question. We may be asking the person to build us up or we may want to hear only a positive response and not the actual truth. For example, if a wife asks her husband how he likes her new dress, does he have the freedom to give his honest (and tactful) opinion? Or is his wife really saying, "Tell me I look nice, tell me I look good, and tell me you like the dress." That is a dishonest question. He should have the freedom to express what he honestly feels and thinks. The principle here is that *all questions should be responded to at face value*. No attempt should be made to read anything into the question and try to figure out the hidden meaning.

How might we do this with our children? Did you ever ask your children how they liked the new meal or the vegetables? If you got upset when they said they didn't like it, what were you really expecting? Probably a positive response. Why get upset when they respond honestly to your question? If you ask your child, "Don't you want to go?" and he says "no," you can still be firm and say he must go, without exploding over the fact that he responded honestly to your question.

How does your child feel when you are going to go to a friend's for dinner and you program him ahead of time by saying, "Now be sure you tell them how good dinner was and how much you liked the meal"? How do you know that he will like it, or that you will like it for that matter? They might serve all of his unfavorite foods. What else could you suggest that he say in order to show courtesy and politeness? You can tell people that you appreciate coming to dinner or appreciate the meal, or select one item that we really did like and comment on that. This may seem like a minor point, but it is important. Your child can learn to discriminate and select an item that he does respond favorably to instead of griping about everything or lying just to please others.

It is amazing how many family members have continued certain behaviors or prepared certain dishes because they thought others really enjoyed them. Years later they discovered that the other person really didn't enjoy them but had continued to give the impression that he did. A wife one time shared what she did with her husband when she cooked him a new recipe. She asked how he liked it and when he said that he did, she then asked, "Well, do you like it enough for me to serve it a second time?" The answer she received at that moment gave her the full extent of his feelings. You need to learn to express your likes and dislikes in a positive manner so your children have a healthy pattern and model.

As parents you are concerned about truthfulness in your children. What you might see as lying on the part of another person (child or adult!) may be a matter of a difference of opinion or another point of view. Truth sometimes lies in the eye of the beholder. You want a child to be accurate. But what is accuracy? What is it to you and what is it for your child? A child will see and evaluate depending on his abilities, and he could miss some of the details. A child's feelings about another person may influence his version of the truth. If he likes or fears another, this will have an effect. The power that parents hold over a child may force him to share partial truths, but it does not always bring out the full truth. Consider what a child thinks about when faced with telling the truth. "What will happen if I don't tell the truth? What will happen if I am found out? What will happen if I do tell the truth?" When a child tells the truth remember that he is telling it the way he saw or experienced it and not necessarily the way that you want him to tell it.

Fantasy and Reality

As a child develops, becoming aware of the differences between fantasy and reality, and gaining the ability to recognize the truth and not to lie, can be a long process. Parents of young children often enjoy playing fantasy games with their child. They pretend with their child about playmates and animals and stories. A few years later, however, he lies about hitting his sister or spilling the paint on the floor. Here a child needs to learn the difference between pretending for fun and lying to escape unpleasant consequences. As a child grows he begins with imagination and fantasy that conceals and distorts true reality. His imagination is very important and will be useful to him throughout his life. Adults can distinguish between what they dreamed and what they feel while awake. You know the difference between senses perception and imagination. Not so for a young child. Truth to him is still fuzzy and is partially controlled by what he can perceive.

If a three-year-old draws a brown swatch on a piece of paper and says that it is a house with animals and people in it, he isn't lying. His account of truth is still influenced by his imagination. A child by the age of four or five begins to understand the possibility of lying to avoid what he doesn't like or want, and he learns how to manipulate the truth for his own benefit. He is learning what is true and what isn't true as well. How do you react when you feel the child has definitely lied? For some parents it is almost the unforgivable sin. A harsh punishment is dealt out to the child. If your child begins to believe that you have a low opinion of him, then he may continue to lie and give up trying to be truthful.

Search for Truth

As parents, you can assist in developing a child who is truthful. This can be done by consistently telling him the truth on his own level. The promises that you make to him should be possible to keep. If because of an emergency one must be broken, he needs an explanation as to the reason and what arrangements can be made to substitute for it. Learning about truth in the home will happen as the child learns to trust you, and as he learns to trust himself, which will come from your trusting him. If your child can understand the consequences of a lie and still feel that you trust him, he will have a better feeling and sense of security about himself and be less apt to repeat that behavior.

The truth is easier to bring out from a child when he is allowed to tell it his own way. If a child is alert and mature and is a good perceiver, the better equipped he is to tell the truth. If you intimidate the child or engage in a power struggle with him in order to find the truth, there will be a defensiveness or resistance on his part. If there is a fear reaction he may, because of the fear, forget parts of the story and you may tend to feel that he is purposely covering up or lying.

Often a search for the truth turns into a debate and a quarrel with very little resolved. If there is evidence of an out-and-out falsehood, appropriate correction and discipline should be exercised. But in matters of opinions where the truth of the matter is not that obvious, there needs to be more discussion so each can begin to learn about the other person's point of view.

How can this be done without everyone becoming overly defensive? To see another person's point of view when a difference of opinion occurs depends on a person's willingness to give up that position long enough to move mentally to the position of the other person. It also means that your goal is understanding the other rather than winning! If you are willing to see your child's position from his point of view, he must realize that by doing this, you are not agreeing with him. And it works the other way as well. If your child is willing to look at the issue from your point of view, do not assume that he agrees with you. Neither of you may change your point of view, but you may gain a greater understanding of each other.

Learning from Questions

Parents ask questions. Children ask questions. A question can be a rich learning experience. You can learn so much about your children by drawing out what is going on inside of them. To involve another person in a conversation, you ask a question. A question invites a reply and is a stimulus for conversation to begin. When you ask your child a question, he understands that you want to know something about what he has been doing or thinking or feeling.

What words do you use to begin your questions? Let's assume that your child has just come home from Sunday School and you would like to know what the class was about. Here are examples of the types of questions you could ask.

Did your class do anything special today, John?
What did you do in your class?
Where is your class going this Saturday?
Why did your class go into the auditorium today?
Who went with you?
How can you tell when your teacher is happy?
How do you feel when you are asked a question? What goes on inside of your mind? Take time right now and think about your response to these questions.

Some people feel threatened. They wonder what will happen if they don't know the answer. Some feel pressured. Others feel challenged. When you or your child is asked a question, you must review your experiences and organize your thoughts. That is why questions are so valuable for the mind development of a child. Questions also stimulate a child to use words more accurately and become more effective in the expression of his ideas. Your questions will help you know what your child observes, thinks, and feels.

In conversation with your child, remember to maintain a balance between questions and statements. Too many questions can overwhelm a child and threaten him. They can actually close off conversation if he becomes fearful. Too many questions may imply that the child does not have his own private world. And if the questions come faster than he can think, then frustration occurs.

Kinds of Questions

Basically there are three types of questions: information, opinion or judgment, and feeling. An *information question* asks another person to share something about his experiences. You ask these when you want the person to share what he has learned, observed, heard or done. Unfortunately many of our information questions call for only a short-answer response, and parents have a tendency to use too many of these. This type of question skims the surface and doesn't really allow you to know the other person. If the child feels as though he is getting the third degree, or being interrogated, he may become angry, moody, or silent, and tune you out.

Information questions should ask for thoughts and an expansion on the subject. "Tell me what happened at your party." "What did you see at school today?" Both of these questions ask for information. You may receive a short or lengthy response. If you were to say, however, "Tell me the finest thing that happened at your party and describe the costumes of six of the people," or "What are ten things that you saw at school today?" you may receive a wealth of information. These last two questions may be better suited for those who are less responsive than for the talkative child. Information questions are usually the first ones you use, for they give you facts before you proceed into opinions, feelings, or emotions.

Opinion and/or judgment questions ask a child to tell what he thinks about something. You are now focusing on ideas. These questions often come from the information derived from information questions. These could also involve "what if" questions as you ask him to think about the future. Think of five different types of opinion questions that you use or could use with your child.

Do these questions call for a short or a long response? Will you ask for a yes-or-no response? For example, if you ask a person, "Is it true?" you will receive a Yes or No. If you ask, "Why do you think it is true?" or "Why is it false?" you will receive a different answer to your questions.

This category of questions is important as you are digging for the meaning and significance of things. You are also helping your child think through future consequences, to prepare him for the future. You need these questions to know what your child is learning and whether he is really in touch with reality.

The third category of questions concerns *feelings*. These questions are crucial to the emotional and mental health of your child. They deal with his fears, worries, anxieties, frustrations, joys, and delights. Many of the questions in this category include the word *feel*. "How did you feel about that?" "What do you feel about your test?"

References

1. Adapted from Sven Wahlroos, *Family Communication* (New York: Macmillan Co., 1974), pp. 192-193.
2. The section on nagging is adapted from Norman Wright, *An Answer to Family Communication* (Irvine, Calif.. Harvest House, 1977), pp. 44-50.